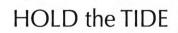

HOLD the TIDE

HOLD the TIDE

a novel

Linnea Lentfer

Rocfish Press
Gustavus, Alaska

Published by Rocfish Press
P.O. Box 162, Gustavus, AK 99826

Library of Congress Control Number: 2021910883
ISBN Number: 978-0-578-88744-9

Book Design: Carolyn Servid
Sitka Willow Consulting | Editing | Design
sitkawillow.com

Cover Photo of Annika Schwartz by Hank Lentfer

Printed in the United States of America
IngramSpark

A WORD OF THANKS

Eve's story is entirely fictional. Yet this book was born from relationships with real people and places. I give my deepest thanks to the following:

To the wet and wondrous Southeast Alaska rainforest and the creatures who share it with me. They've filled my life with beauty, purpose and meaning.

To Bob Christensen for welcoming me to his home on Tàaś Daa from my first visit as a diapered bundle of baby fat through my teens. His generosity has shaped me and this story in more ways than I can describe.

To Iris White for letting me claim her as a sister and inspiring me daily with her grit, talent, and kindness. Eve's story was born from the hours running at her side barefoot on the beach.

To Greg Streveler for his generosity and patience. There is no one I am more honored to call a friend and teacher.

To Dia Calhoun for the hours of editing, meetings, and support that moved Eve from my head and heart onto the page. Without her patience, wisdom, and craft this book would not exist.

To Kim Heacox for reading drafts and all the belly laughs and eleven minute Beatles medleys.

To Tonja Moser for making me a writer in a dozen different ways and gently shoving me into the deep end of every task at hand.

To Jen Gardener for reading drafts and the hours of conversation about story, art, and life in general.

To Carolyn Elder for her generous and careful copy editing.

To Carolyn Servid for her artful eye and skillful layout.

To Anna Iverson and Katie McKenna for constant inspiration, outrageous adventure, and ab-spraining laugh sessions.

To my mother Anya Maier. Everything I am has grown from her unwavering love and support.

To Hank Lentfer for being a best friend, loving parent, and sharing the craft of writing. This book would not have been possible without him inspiring me to get off my butt, encouraging me through the teeth-pulling parts of crafting stories, and sharing countless mornings quietly chasing words.

ONE

The wood stove door creaks. I open my eyes and see Mama blowing gently on last night's coals. I roll over, my tangled mat of hair scratching my neck. Mama adds a bit of tinder, moving slowly, trying not to wake me. I close my eyes again, breathing in the familiar scent of the deer-hide blankets.

The smell of burning moss tickles my nose as the fire begins to catch. Mama adds twigs, then larger branches. The stove squeaks again. She takes the pot from the stove, slides on her boots, and steps outside, the door thumping softly behind her. As her footsteps fade, a raven croaks. Wind brushes spruce branches against the tin roof. A squirrel chatters and then skitters across the back cabin wall. The fire crackles and pops, coming to life.

I open my eyes and look for shapes in the gnarled wood paneling. I look here so much I've already found all the hidden shapes. My favorite is the squirrel, her beady eye a dark knot staring me right in the face.

Mama comes back and sets the tea water on the stove. She picks up the half-finished shirt, edging close to the window for more light. I watch as she pokes the needle through the stiff deer hide and pulls it out with the pliers. Before we found them on the beach last year, it would take us twice as long to sew any hide, the needle was so hard to get through from the back. Mama breaks off the sinew thread and ties a knot. I let my eyes fall shut and burrow into the pillow.

The tea water gurgles and chuckles as it boils. Mama sets down the shirt and comes over to the stove. I sit up. She jumps back, almost knocking the pot onto the floor.

"Eve!" she laughs, "I had no idea you were awake."

"I've been watching you since you went out to the creek."

"And you were too lazy to get up and help me?" she teases.

I smile. She pours tea into our cups. I lean against the wall and take my cup from her. Steam wafts up and condenses on my chin.

Mama takes a sip of tea and wraps her hands around the wooden cup. It's the perfect shape: her fingers curl all the way around just touching at the tips. Samuel and I made it in secret last fall when he was stuck on the Island with a northerly. Mama's had her tea in it every morning since.

"Eve?"

I snap my eyes away from her cup and look up. Mama grins. "Want to dig potatoes today?"

I nod so vigorously I almost spill my tea. It's the perfect day for it.

"I thought you might like that."

She takes a long drink, then sets her cup down on the hearth. I lean back against the wall and pull the bed skins tighter around my shoulders.

Mama tussles my hair. I flinch away. She takes a mat of curls between her fingers and spreads it out, examining the tangles.

"You didn't brush your hair yet, did you?"

I turn away from her, twisting a reddish blond strand around my finger.

"I told you to brush it yesterday morning." She runs her hand over the mat of curls. "If you'd just brush it often enough, then it would never get so bad. Let me work on it." She picks up the comb and works it through the snarls. I turn my head and snatch my hair over my shoulder.

"I can brush my own hair!"

"Not so as you'd notice."

"Mama, I'm not a baby. I can take care of myself. I could even cut my hair off if I wanted to."

Mama sighs. "But how could you cut your hair? It's red-gold and it goes almost to your waist now. There isn't another girl alive who..." Mama clamps her mouth shut.

"What do you mean 'another girl'?"

Mama cuts back in before I can finish.

"Eve, if you'd just brush it then…"

I roll my eyes. "…then it would never be this bad. But if I just cut it then I will never have to brush it."

"Wild child. Just brush your hair. If you start now you can finish faster than it took us to argue about it. Okay?"

I reach down to the hearth where Mama put a bucket of cranberries for breakfast. The sour makes me cough. Mama laughs. I try to keep a straight face but my mouth breaks into a smile.

"Well, I'll go get the bucket," Mama says. "Come find me at the potato bed."

I nod and eat another handful of cranberries, then wash the sour down with the last gulp of tea. The spruce branches scrape across the tin roof again. I push the deer skin off my shoulders and pull on my long underwear and wool skirt from their pile on the floor. I can feel the grit of dirt and clay on my legs as I pull them on. Sometimes when Mama's get dirty she washes them in the creek. I don't mind the grit though. It's "an extra layer" like Uncle Samuel says.

My hair gets pressed against my back as I slide my sweater over my head. I can feel the thickness of the mats against my bare skin. I tug the tangled mat out and look at the ends. A bit of spruce bark is caught in the curls.

I flick it off, sending it sliding off the top of the stove then onto the hearth.

The wind snaps my skirt as I walk down the path to the potato patch. Sun peaks through the trees scattering little pieces of light on the moss. I don't have to look at my feet, I know each root by heart. The dogwood leaves are just rimmed with the first lines of brown from fall.

I duck out of the alders and step over the three long rows of potato hills. Mama's at the other end pulling up the plants. The buckets sit empty at my feet. Her back must be hurting already, otherwise she would have filled them. I take the buckets to the water's edge. The tide is halfway out, just to the edge of the barnacles. I press the rim of each bucket under water until they're a quarter full and haul them towards Mama. My hair falls over my shoulders. I stop, twist it into one long rope and tuck it in my sweater. Maybe Mama won't notice that I haven't brushed it.

I reach the rows and set the buckets down. They slosh in a circle but they're not full enough to spill.

Mama stands.

"Thanks," she says. She wipes the dirt from the sloppy, rotting potato stems on the gravel and puts her arm around my shoulder. I rest my cheek on her arm. A chilly gust blows across the water and onto our backs, snapping my tangled hair over my shoulder.

Mama squats down and pulls out a plant, shaking the gravel and kelp off the stem. I plop the first three potatoes in the bucket and wriggle my hands in for more. We fall into a rhythm: pull, dig, plop. The beach gravel is cold, and my hands become covered in kelp, but I don't mind.

Once we finish five hills, Mama stamps down a place in the grass and I carry each bucket over. We dump them out and use moss to rub off the last bits of kelp. Wind rattles the alders, sending leaves dancing down the beach. My hair blows around, twirling in front of my face.

Up on the ridge, three Vs of birds soar above me, the wind at their backs. They're so loud that I can hear them through the wind.

"Cranes!" I yell, pointing.

Mama scans the sky until she finds them, then smiles back at me. The flock molds back and forth, keeping a loose V formation. I run down the beach to get a better view. Mama walks over the rocks to join me. Her foot slides on a piece of kelp and she presses her hand to her lower back. I lift my arms up toward the birds.

The leader of the flock disappears over the ridge. Soon they are all out of sight and their chortling calls blow away in the wind.

Mama looks back at me. "It's good to see them again. It seems like a long time ago they flew over in the spring."

I nod. "Where do they go?"

Mama looks away, tucks her hair behind her ear and looks back.

"The only way to find out where they go is ask the cranes."

I sigh. "That's what you say every year. What's on the other side of the ridge?"

"I don't know."

"But you know where Uncle Samuel goes. You've been around the reef before. You've seen the other side of the ridge."

Mama's face is pinched. She looks over the water, out to the shore on the other side of the strait. White caps are sprinkled like spilled grains of rice. The ridge across the strait is dark green, almost black against the grey sky.

Mama turns back to me.

"Sweetie, I'm...you have to trust me. Being here is better than anything where Samuel lives. Since you don't have to miss the other world, then you can be happy here."

I look at her.

"But Mama..." Tears push at the corners of my eyes. *Don't cry now. Not now.* "Why don't you let me know!"

She puts her arms around my shoulders. "Oh, Wild Child..."

I jerk away.

"Eve!"

I run up the beach and leap over the just-dug hills. I trip over one of the buckets, sloshing muddy water on the back of my legs. I know what Mama looks like behind me, wind whipping her hair. Her face trying to be angry but only looking sad and hurt. I don't look back.

I sit on the cabin steps and let my breath slow down. Mama will come up the path soon. She will pull me close and, whether I want to or not, I will start to cry. She will run her hand over my hair and not say anything. Then when I stop Mama will make a joke and we will both laugh and then go back and finish the potatoes. Tonight, she will brush my hair no matter what I do.

I walk into the cabin and sit on the bed. My hair rolls over my shoulder and swings in front of my face. Our knife sits on the hearth, next to the sharpening stone. I pick it up and touch my thumb to the blade. It needs to be touched up, but it's sharp enough for now. I slide the leather sheath over the knife and tuck it in the waistband of my skirt.

Outside, I rub my arms against the wind. I slide along the side of the cabin, in between the brush and the grey cedar siding. A raven croaks from the top of the cotton-wood above the creek. Spruce needles pull at my skirt. I pass the back of the woodshed and tuck under the low branches to my tree cave. This is the only place where

Mama or even Samuel has never been. It's just for me. I can see the porch and the meat cache through the branches, but Mama can't see me, unless she crawls on the ground behind the wood shed.

I sit on my spruce root and slide the knife out of my pocket. The wood has been worn smooth from me sitting on it. Just by my head there is a hole in the bark where my hair always gets stuck in the dripping sap. I pick up the bottom of a bouncy curl and stretch it out as far as I can. It reaches just past my waist.

A squirrel scampers up a tree, chattering nonstop. Maybe she can use my hair for her nest. I picture her babies snuggled into it. I grab a handful of hair and cut upwards. It floats to the ground. I watch it land on the moss.

I did it.

I grab another handful and cut. And another. And another. The knife snips with each one. I lean my head forward and cut the back. I hack at the other side then trim the top.

My head feels so light! I toss it back and forth. The wind dances through the trees and hits my bare neck. The hair lying on the moss seems so thin and small compared to what it felt like on my head. I push out of the trees and back to the cabin.

Mama will be here any minute. I stand on the porch before walking towards the creek. It doesn't matter what

Mama thinks. It's my hair. She'll probably be glad that I don't have to brush it anymore.

The wind is cold but sun peeks through the trees. My head is so light that I feel like I could float above the Island, I could fly off with the cranes. I could look back down on the cabin and the potatoes and have them be so small that I could hold up my hand and they would disappear underneath it. The wind would spill over my face and I would fly so high I could see the other side of the Island. Could see where Samuel is. Where flour and rice and sugar come from.

I would fly away from the Island. I would fly until my hair grew back in and I would float down into the yard and come to the cabin door and tell Mama about everything on the other side of the ridge.

TWO

The musty, wet, red smell of cranberries fills every corner of the cabin. I squish the berries around, their plump, red-orange skin bursting, squirting juice everywhere.

Mama adjusts the drying rack, a loosely woven mat of spruce root with branches around the perimeter, and then starts mixing beside me. I tuck my hair behind my ears. Mama hasn't said anything about it since I cut it ten days ago. I squirm whenever she looks my way.

"That's probably about as squished as we want them," she says, lifting up a handful of the red-orange pulp. "We want as much juice as we can in the cakes."

I wrinkle my nose. "That juice makes it more sour."

Mama laughs. "Oh, the juice is the best part."

I smile. "Only when you put enough sugar on it."

"We don't have any left for this batch. You'll have to suffer through."

"We have a little."

Mama brushes bits of dried pulp off the back of her hands.

"Yes, but we'll have to save it."

"Why can't we wait until Uncle Samuel comes with more?"

Mama turns away. She slams her fists open and closed in the berries, smashing the pulp into a square cake.

"Why *hasn't* he come yet, Mama?"

Mama slaps her cake onto the rack.

"There's no telling when he will come."

She sighs, then plunges her hands back in the pot of berry pulp. I try to stick my hair behind my ear with… what? A clump of cranberry pulp. It stays for a moment and then falls down again. The front always falls in my face now.

"What do you mean?" I ask.

Mama finishes mashing the berries into a cake and slaps them onto the rack. It swings backward on the woodstove, clanging into the stack.

I try again. "The wind's been good for the past few weeks. Why wouldn't he come before the fall storms start?"

Mama attacks the berry pulp again. "I don't know. How could I know living here?"

I clamp my hand around the rack so it stops swinging.

"Is something wrong there? Where he lives?"

Mama looks up at me. Her hands stop mashing the berries.

"I don't know, sweetie," she says, softly.

I keep working at the berry cake in my hands. I can tell Mama doesn't know more. Not that she would tell me if she did. I finish forming the cake and lay it on the rack next to Mama's.

"Eve."

"Yes?"

"You know what to do if you ever see a boat, right?"

"Yes, I know."

"Tell me."

I sigh. "It doesn't matter that I think it is Samuel, that I know it's Samuel. Until he does his call, I have to go to our hiding spot."

"And stay there until..." Mama prompts.

"I *know*, Mama. You've made me say it a thousand times."

"Then tell me."

"I stay there until he does his owl hoot and then I'm still careful until I know it's him."

"Good." Mama squeezes my shoulder. "Now let's dump the last bit of that sugar on." She grins. "There's nothing worse than a berry cake too sour to eat."

🌾

The smell of cranberry steam coats every surface. It saturates each hair of the bed skins around me. Or maybe it's just me smelling that way. I turn to rub my nose in Mama's hair to get the smell out. Her spot is empty. She must be out at the creek. But she got water yesterday.

I sit up. She's not in the cabin at all. A full sack of sugar lies on the hearth. Samuel's here!

I throw off the bed skins. The chilly air wraps around my bare legs, but I don't mind. I pull on my long underwear and my skirt over the top, then put my jacket on over my blouse.

I clomp down the cabin steps and run to the beach. The wind has come up, snapping my short mass of hair around my ears.

I break out of the trees and onto the beach. The boat is pulled up to the dolphin right next to the rock. Mama hoists a sack of rice from under the tarp in the bottom of the bow. Samuel slides the rollers out from under the seat and begins to set them up to haul the boat into the grass.

"Uncle Samuel!" I call.

He turns his head. "Wild Child!" he booms. His beard and hair have gotten more grey than blond but otherwise he looks just the same as he did in the spring. I run toward him.

Mama looks up at me. Her hair is brushed and braided already. Her arms stick out of the sleeves of her coat— she left the biggest, warmest one in the cabin for me.

Her back must feel better, too; she's carrying a sack of rice on her shoulder and walking straighter than usual.

Samuel sets the rollers down and holds his arms out for a hug. Mama looks up at him. Samuel lowers his arms. I look at Mama. Her face is hard.

"Eve!" Her voice is so sharp it makes me shrink. "What do you think you're doing here?"

I look from Samuel and back to Mama.

The call. Samuel didn't do the call yet.

"I just came down to see him, Mama! There was a sack of sugar on the hearth, I knew he was here, I knew you were outside helping him. And I was right!"

Mama puts her hands on my shoulders. Her voice is softer, but I can tell she's still mad. "Whether or not you think it's Samuel, or you know it's Samuel, always hide when you hear a boat. Always. And stay there until I come get you or Samuel calls. And you just came running down here without a care in the world. I thought you could remember, Eve."

"Mama, of course I remember! But it just doesn't make sense!"

"It doesn't take long. I'd find you right after you hide."

I look over at Uncle Samuel. He moves his eyes away from me to Mama.

"But why do I have to hide? There's never been a boat here other than Samuel's. The only thing close was that boat in the strait last summer."

Samuel's mouth drops open, then he shakes his head. "Sarah, you never told me they..."

Mama turns to look at him and he stops.

"Eve," she says, still with her hands on my shoulders. "I know it doesn't really make sense now, but hiding from boats is more important than ever right now."

"Now why don't you give your poor Uncle a hug?" Samuel says. "He's just over here doing all the work and you haven't said as much as hello."

I want to know more. I don't want to hide. But instead I wrap my arms around Samuel. He smells the same as always. The same dusty sweet of what he calls tobacco. He picks me up and throws me into the air, just like he did when I was five. I laugh, and just for a second I feel like I could fly with the cranes and look at Samuel's world. And never have to hide again.

Once all the food is hauled into the cabin and the extra sacks are stored away in the meat cache, Mama starts soaking rice for dinner. I add bits of dried salmon and kelp for the rice to soak up flavor. We never add two flavorings unless we have an epically big salmon run or if Samuel's here.

"You should go get Samuel's fiddle," Mama whispers in my ear. "If he's not helping us make dinner, then he might as well play some music."

I smile. "Where is it?"

"In his bag. Behind where we put the flour."

I go over to the corner and reach behind the pile of sacks. I dig around until I feel the oiled canvas under my fingers, then pull it out and bring it to Samuel. He smiles.

"You never forget about the music, do you?"

Mama and I smile at each other.

"You might as well make yourself useful," I say.

He laughs. "I guess I'd better play, then."

He opens the draw string and lays the instrument on the bed. I brush my fingers over the curve in the scroll. Samuel rubs rosin into the bow.

"You gave those wild curls a little trim, didn't you, Wild Child?"

It's the first time anyone has talked about the haircut. I glance at Mama but she's facing into the pot of rice. I nod back at Samuel.

"Suits you," he says, the fiddle between his beard and his shoulder. "Now you look so wild that you just might fly away."

I grin. Somehow, Samuel always knows what to say.

He bounces the bow across the strings. "What do you want to hear?" he asks.

"Anything!" I almost shout. Mama smiles at me. "Anything fast."

"All right then." He plays a long A-Flat. He bends his arm back to turn the peg. I listen until he has the pitch perfect. He and Mama taught me to hear the notes years ago. *When the note bounces back and forth like this, that means it's not quite right. You just move this peg a teensy bit this way or that way until the sound is smooth.*

Once he finishes tuning he plays a few quick notes.

"Not quite," says Mama. "The E is still a little sharp."

Samuel turns the peg down until the note is perfectly smooth.

"You always had the best ear, Sarah," he says. "I never would have heard that."

"But I could never play to save my life," Mama laughs. "I used to be so jealous of you."

I nudge Samuel. He grins. "All right then. No point sitting around tuning is there?"

He puts the bow on the strings and lets his fingers fly. Mama starts tapping her foot. She smiles into the soup pot. I sit and watch Samuel's bow. The music fills me up. So full it seems like it flows outside of me, outside of the cabin, off away from the Island, to all the corners of the world where the cranes fly.

After dinner, Mama pulls out the spruce baskets from the corner. Our biggest one lost its bottom in the summer so we need a new one. I don't have a tight enough weave to make a berry basket but I take the snarl of roots from the pile and peel their bark off with my fingernail. Mama lights a candle from the woodstove, sending light dancing along the walls. She sits on the other side of the hearth.

Samuel goes to get his bedding from the boat. A gust of wind blows down the chimney and rain hisses in the fire. The storm makes the cabin feel safe and warm. I pull the deerskin from the bed around my shoulders. The storm means Samuel will stay. I watch the light from the candle dance back and forth. My eyes close.

The door squeaks as Samuel comes in. He puts his bed skins down in the corner, then pours himself a cup of tea from the stove.

"She's fast asleep, isn't she," he says looking over at me.

Mama shifts so she can see me. "Yep. All worn out."

The floorboards creak as Samuel eases down next to Mama. He sighs.

"Sarah, even if it's still blowing I've got to go tomorrow."

Mama takes a sharp breath in. There's a long pause.

"Samuel, the waves are breaking. You can't go."

What? Why would he go? With the waves breaking he wouldn't make it past the reef!

"I know, Sarah. I'm not stupid. But there's been three escapes in the last two years. That's too many supplies to hide, much less buy. We need another family but you can't just go around asking. That's why I couldn't come before now. If I'm not back before Monday, well...you know."

I twist my fingers around the roots in my hand. The other people in Samuel's world. Supplies. Why would they have to hide them? What does it mean to buy?

Mama's voice is fast and high. It's the same tone she uses when she is afraid that the bear is looting our snares. "But they wouldn't do more than search, would they?" she asks. "And if they do find one cabin what's to tell them there's another? I know the society. Better than most people. I'll never forget. But isn't Eve still the only child? Couldn't the others escape again?"

Everything whirls around in my head. Search? Only child? And what makes Mama so afraid? It's more than Samuel going out in the storm.

"Sarah, you know they are always looking for something more to do than sew frills on their uniforms." Samuel's voice is loud, not in a laughing way.

"Shhhh," Mama hisses. Samuel keeps going in a hard whisper.

"If they find one cabin, they're going to look for more. Besides the fact that I'd be in jail and Pa can't row out here anymore. And what if they find your cabin first? What if, as soon as I'm not back, they come out here and haul Eve away and she doesn't even know why?" Samuel's voice cracks. "I know that we try to stay safe.

But really, if they get on to us, there's nothing to stop them from coming here. I think you forget, Sarah. I think that you don't remember that people are a lot crueler than any storm you'll ever see."

I wrap the spruce roots tighter around my hands. I don't understand. But I know it's not good. And I know that it's not anything that they want me to hear.

"I'll never let them take Eve. Ever." Mama says fiercely. "I'll go first and they won't know she's there."

"Yes, but if they find the cabin, we're powerless. We can't ever let them out here. I've got to be back by Monday. Or die trying."

"Samuel..." Mama's voice trails off. Uncle Samuel sighs. I hear the snip of Mama's knife as she tapers off the end of a root and adds another one to the basket. Samuel can't leave, there's no way he can get around the reef. But who are the other people? The ones they are so afraid of? I can feel tears moving down my face but if I move to brush them away, they'll know I'm awake.

❦

No one says anything as we haul the boat down the beach the next morning. When I told them at breakfast that I heard them talking last night Mama gasped but didn't say anything. Samuel squeezed my shoulder and said, "I guess you understand a little better why I need to go then." I only nodded.

Wind blows past my ears and tugs at my hair. Mama holds onto the boat for a moment before setting it down. I wish she could keep it there, suspended above the gravel until the wind dies down. I wish that I could keep this morning going forever.

I lower the oars into the boat and look over the water. The strait is choppy, scattered with white caps. The sky is dull gray, low on the water. The head of a seal bobs in and out of sight with the swell. Uncle Samuel turns to me and opens his arms. I hug him. He squeezes me tight. His beard scratches my cheek.

"I'll see you next time, Wild Child."

"You'll come back, right?" I ask. My forehead is pressed against his neck. I can feel him swallow.

"I promise," he whispers.

I nod and hug him tighter. He rubs my back then lets me go and reaches into the boat.

"Take care of this for me, Eve."

He hands me his fiddle. "I don't want it getting too wet on the run and next time I come, *you* can play for *me*."

I hug the sack to my chest. "I promise I'll take good care of it."

"Samuel, are you sure..." Mama asks.

"Yes, Sarah. You know I have to go. Asking only makes it harder." He looks at Mama, back at me, then at Mama again. "For all of us."

She hugs him.

"Promise me you'll be careful."

"Promise me you'll tell Eve."

"I'll tell her when I need to. I'll tell her when it's time."

"Now is the time, Sarah. And after what she heard last night, it must be scarier *not* knowing the truth," says Samuel.

He hugs Mama one more time, then we all lean over to secure the tarp in the bow. He pushes the boat into the waves and jumps to the oars. I take Mama's hand. We watch as the boat grows smaller and smaller till it crests over a wave and my eyes lose track of it in a mess of blue-black water and white foam.

"He'll be all right, won't he?" I ask.

"If anyone can make it through that water, your Uncle Samuel can."

I turn to look at Mama. "Mama, will you tell me?"

She just holds on to my hand tighter and looks out over the water. When she answers it is only a whisper towards the waves.

"Yes. Yes, I will."

THREE

Wind charges through the trees. Even next to the cabin, I hear the waves crash onto the beach, then the boom of the next one while the water is still sizzling out. I pull the saw back in rhythm with Mama, down into the spindly spruce trunk. We haven't said anything to each other since Samuel left this morning.

"Mama?"

She nods.

"You said you would tell me."

Mama just keeps the rhythm of the saw, her face pointed down at the wood. I let go of my side of the handle. Mama pulls backward and the saw jerks towards her. She stands and looks at me.

"Mama, you said you would!" A gust of wind roars through the trees, snapping Mama's hair across her face. "Please. Samuel wants you to."

She nods, and mumbles something. I pick up my end of the saw and we keep cutting. The round we've been cutting falls onto the frozen moss. Mama picks up the saw and starts another cut. I count the times the saw passes back and forth between us. One, two ...five.

"Eve, where Samuel lives people are everywhere." Her voice is soft, but sure. She keeps her eyes on the wood and the saw's motion between us.

"There are more people than there are gulls in the flock at the beach. They live in cabins right next to each other. Except the cabins are bigger. They're called houses. Believe it or not, I was born in one of them. A house on 5th Street."

I stare up at Mama. Our cabin is so big it can hold almost all our dry food, and the bed, and the woodstove. What would someone do with more space than that? And more people than gulls on the beach? I picture the people covering the shore like seagulls, talking and yammering to each other.

Mama looks up at me and smiles. Then focuses back down at the log.

"Our house wasn't very big for a house but it was at least three times the size of this cabin. There were two stories, like one cabin stacked on another. There was a cookstove, too, and it was warm all the time." She pauses. I push on the saw, buckling it in the wood. Mama lifts it out, then places it back in straight.

I try to imagine a cabin balanced on the top of another one, the floor perched on the roof's peak. "How could you cut enough wood to keep a house like that warm?"

"We burned coal instead of firewood. My papa would come home with sacks of it. Just like the sacks that Uncle Samuel brings. And he'd just have to give a few pieces of paper for a whole sack. It would burn all week and whenever we ran out, we could just go and get another." She sighs.

Questions are bubbling up inside of me. What would it be like if our firewood lasted that long? We probably wouldn't even have to cut wood at all. I could chop kindling once every week instead of every morning.

Mama chuckles. "I didn't even know *how* to cut firewood back then." There is a hint of a smile in her voice but it still sounds serious.

"Life there was so different. Our house was always full of people. My mama and my papa were there. My mama's sister, aunt Elizabeth, lived with us, too. Every Sunday our friends and neighbors would come to our house for dinner. We weren't rich but we had so much food we never could get hungry. Samuel and I and all the other children would run and laugh and play together. And after dinner, there was always music. I remember that best of all. I would curl up next to my mama while she sang and watch everyone else play. I..."

Mama's voice breaks off. She pushes on the saw making it buckle. I try to pull it out, but she drops the handle and picks up the rounds that we have already cut.

"That's enough wood for now, Eve," she says. "Let's bring this to the shed."

"But Mama! What about Samuel? What about…?"

"Not now, Eve," Mama calls. She's already walking away towards the shed. I start to run to follow her and trip over the rest of the wood. How can Mama just walk away? How could she have never told me about any of this before?

I bend down and lift a few rounds, cradling them in my bent arm. I've asked Mama questions since I could first talk. Asked her about the rest of the world away from the cabin. But she never told me about what was really there.

Two rounds clatter out of my arms. I pick them up and follow Mama to the woodshed. She never even said what Samuel had been talking about. Why he had to go. As I near the shed Mama walks back towards the cabin and closes the door.

❧

I sit cross-legged and stare into the flames. Mama's face is hidden in shadows. She holds the spruce root basket close to the fire. Her hands flash in and out of the light, as she wraps the roots around the warp. I slide the knife down the top of a root, and peel the edge off, leaving it naked light yellow with its smooth, wet coating. The wind moans outside. Through the smudged glass on the woodstove door, the flames scurry around the logs, eating their way into the wood's center.

Wind blows rain down the chimney. The fire hisses. Just like last night when Samuel was here. He might still be on the water now. Who knows where? I imagine him hunched in the rain. The waves breaking over the bow of the boat.

Mama tapers the end of the root she is working on with her knife. She has hardly said anything since we gathered the wood this morning.

"Mama?"

"Yes?"

"You…You haven't told me anything yet. And you promised Samuel."

"What do you mean?" She asks.

I slam my knife's handle onto the hearth. Mama jumps.

"You stopped right in the middle! You never said why I have to hide. Why Samuel had to go." I stare through the shadows at Mama's face. She scrapes a fleck of bark off the root with her fingernail.

"I'm sorry, sweetie," she says." I know it's time for you to know. But I haven't said anything for so long…it's not easy to tell you all of a sudden."

I open my mouth to say something more. But Mama cuts me off.

"They took me away from it all. From my family, from the music, from everything. I haven't been in that house since I was your age."

Light and shadow from the fire leap up and down along the walls. I'm usually comforted by the shadows, but not now.

"What do you mean taken away?"

"It's sort of like the crows on our beach." Mama's voice is soft, controlled again. She reaches forward and picks up the basket. "If they think one of their own isn't right, they'll turn on them. The other people there, where Samuel lives, turn on their own all the time. The guards didn't like me because of the curve in my back."

I push onto my knees.

"Why? What's wrong with that?"

Mama tucks another strand of warp in between two roots. "They said it would make me too weak."

But Mama's so strong! She can drag deer, and carry sacks of flour and rice. And she can sew deer hide and pick berries twice as fast as I can!

"But it doesn't!" I say.

Mama looks straight at the basket in her lap. Her voice sounds flat and far away. "They called it Imperfection. After my fifth yearly checkup, the examiner told us I was an Imperfect. I had to go in every month to get looked at. As soon as I started to get breasts they took me away and locked me up with all the other people they called Imperfect."

Mama finishes the root. I hand her the next one. She sounds far away.

"My aunt Elizabeth took me to that appointment. And after that, they took me straight to the enclosure. They locked me up. I didn't even get a chance to say goodbye to my mama."

"They took you away from your mama!" I try to imagine what I would do without Mama. I breathe in her smell. If she were gone...no, it won't happen. There aren't any other people to take us away. Except Samuel's voice flashes in my head. *Sarah, you know they're always looking for more to do than sew more frills on their uniforms.* I shiver.

Mama takes my hand and puts it on her lap, pushing the basket aside. "I got to see my Mama once a year, but only for two hours. The first few years I clung to my Mama and cried when she left, and the guards would peel me off of her, but soon I stopped fighting. Sometimes I even felt afraid to hug her because I knew it would be so hard to let go."

I hold onto Mama's hand. "Could you see Samuel?"

"No, I couldn't see Samuel or my Papa, there were only women allowed in the enclosure. Except for the guards.

Sometimes the children from the rich families would come to the fence and throw rocks and food at us. To the guards, we were cows. They fed us, and gave us a place to sleep, but we weren't human to them."

The stove gongs as it cools. Shadows are creeping closer as the light from the last few coals fades. Mama's story... seems so far away, so unreal. And so scary at the same time.

"How did you get here?"

"When you started growing in my belly, I escaped. With Samuel helping me. He snuck me out at night in a wheelbarrow. Just as we were leaving the enclosure, a guard almost caught us. Samuel saw his shadow just before he turned the corner. I remember the jolt when he dropped the handles of the wheelbarrow and flattened himself in the grass. The guard walked so close to me I could have reached out and touched him but he never thought I was more than an old wheelbarrow of rags, not a pregnant Imperfect. And Samuel was only seventeen. Risking everything for his little sister."

I pull the skin over my shoulders and hold it with my free hand. Could the guards be who Samuel was afraid of last night? I imagine crows in frilly uniforms coming up the beach.

Mama doesn't say anything more. The roots from the basket drape over the edge of the bed, casting long spidery shadows.

"How did you come here?" I ask.

"I had to hide from the guards. They would have found me that day if I stayed in the town or went back to my house. Samuel took me as far away as he could get me. Out here."

The wind howls. Just yesterday the wind and the rain were all that existed in the world. Just yesterday there were only three people that existed. Just yesterday nothing could be dangerous except for the cold or an animal you misunderstood. Mama pulls me into a hug. I rest my head on her shoulder.

"Why can't we go back, Mama? Couldn't Samuel help you escape again?"

She strokes my hair with the tip of her fingers.

"Eve, there was a reason I had to escape when I was pregnant with you. They didn't allow the Imperfects to have babies. They thought that the babies might be Imperfects too. You are the most perfect human that I've ever seen, sweetie. All they'd do if they found me is toss me around a little and put me back in the enclosure. But if they find out you exist...if they find out where you are..."

Mama clutches me tighter. My ear is pressed into the hard edge of her tunic. Rain drives onto the side of the cabin wall.

"If they find you, Wild Child, they'll kill you."

FOUR

The wind grabs at my hair and whips it around my ears. Waves foam around the rocky point, crashing up and sending sheets of salty mist into my face through the storm. I spread my arms and lean forward. Wind fills my mouth and eyes. It holds me up in a cradle of wet-smelling air, salty spray, and wildness. I smile.

The gust dies. I spin my arms to keep from falling forward into the snow. The tide is too high to walk from shore out to the reef, so I stay on the top of the bedrock cliff. A sea otter watches me from just beyond where the tip of the reef peaks above the waves. A curtain of sky hangs over her in the foaming angry water behind. Around the farthest point of grey land, the water blends in with the sky as a dark threatening mass.

No boats would be able to make it to the Island today.

But since Mama told me about Samuel's world, about the guards like the crows, I come out every day to check.

I turn towards the cabin. Mama will be back from checking the snares soon. Not that we will have caught anything in the snow. Wind blows at the base of my neck, wiping my hair in my eyes. The deer have been pushed down to the beach for almost two weeks now. Last night we had to open the last sack of rice from Samuel.

I turn to the water one last time. A wave sprays up, cutting at the snow's edge, almost drenching my feet. Storms used to scare me. Now they make the cabin feel safe. They're protection against the rest of the world.

It doesn't take me long to run back to the cabin. We covered the windows with boards months ago to keep in the heat, so now the cabin is dim no matter what time of day. I step inside and blink, waiting for my eyes to adjust to the darkness. Mama is bent over the stove, making tea. Her back looks better than it did a few days ago, but she stiffens with pain each time she takes a step. The cold makes things worse.

"Where were you?" she asks when I walk in the door. We are low enough on food that we only drink tea during the day and eat at dinner, but for now tea is good enough. She pours the water into my cup, holding the yarrow back with a spoon.

"Out on the point." I slide off my boots and wrap my stiff fingers around the cup. I haven't told Mama I go out and check for boats. She knows I go out to the reef every day, but she never asks why.

I take a sip of tea. "Any sign in the snares?"

Mama shakes her head. "Nothing new."

I nod. The empty rice sack is shoved in the kindling box for fire starter. I scrunch it down with my foot.

Mama strains the tea leaves out of the water, then goes to dump them off the porch. I lift Samuel's fiddle from where I keep it in the clothes crate, and trace the delicate curve of the f-holes with my first finger. Every day since Samuel left I've cleaned the wood with his special cloth. I tuck the smooth wood under my chin and imagine that I can play like Samuel. Every time I try, it sounds more like an angry blue jay than music.

Mama comes back in and sets the empty pot on the stove. She looks at our other pot with leftover soup. It's mostly water with a little rice and salmon mixed in.

"I don't think we'll be able to add anything to this tonight, sweetie," she says. "With just that last sack of rice..."

"Okay," I say as cheerfully as I can. But I'm already hungry. Watery soup isn't going to be enough to fill me up. I slip the fiddle and the cloth back into the bag and tuck it in the corner of the skins.

Mama sits on the bed. "I know this is a long go without meat, Wild Child. But we've been through it before. And once the snow melts a little more, the deer will come up off the beach onto our snare trails."

I nod again. The rice sack un-scrunches out of the kindling box. I shove it back in with my heel.

"The tides are getting big enough for clams too," Mama says. "We can go out tonight."

I smile. "That's what we always do without meat. Eat rubbery clams all winter long."

Mama laughs. "Yep, that's about right."

◊

I scrape away at the frozen clay. My fingers brush the clam shell's hard edge and I pry it loose. I set it in the basket and look around for other clam squirts. The tide is as low as it gets and the wind has died down so that there's only small choppy waves, a rare thing in winter. I scan the water out by the reef. No disruptions on the horizon. I squint, looking to the farthest stretch of water that I can see before the point of the opposite shore juts out. No boats.

Another clam-squirt catches my eye. Blowing on my numb hands, I walk down the beach and start digging. Mama is in front of me, bent over a different clam. After Mama told me about the Imperfects and the guards, we haven't said anything else about it. Or anything about Samuel. I've never told her that I check for boats out on the reef. Or that I put a basket with an extra bed skin and salmon fillet in the woodshed.

I wrestle loose the clam and lay it in the basket.

"Mama?"

She turns and looks at me. "Umm hmm?"

"If we saw a boat right now. That wasn't Samuel's. What would happen?"

Mama doesn't stop and snap at me like I expected her to. Instead she comes over and puts three more mucky clams in the basket.

"We would hide. If we had time, we would run to the ravine behind the last deer snare. But if we didn't have time, I'm not sure what would happen." She lifts the basket, a silent signal that we have enough, and we start to walk up the beach.

"I don't know what they would do or how long they would search." Mama pauses and adjusts the basket handle in her hand. I take one side and help her carry it.

"As long as you hide, sweetie, you'll be okay. I'll never let them...let them do anything to you. If a boat ever comes, just don't let them see you and you'll be fine."

We reach the edge of the tide-cut snow. I scramble up the steep face and grab my mittens from their nest in the frost. I don't understand the boats. I don't understand why the other people would call Mama an Imperfect, or why they would come to find her again. But now I understand Mama's fear. I shake the snow out of my mitten and pull it on.

"Mama..." I stop. Something at the edge of the water, almost to the point, thrashes. I touch Mama's arm and point.

"What's that?"

Mama sets the basket down in the snow. "I'm not sure. Let's go see."

We turn and make our way back down the beach. Through the growing darkness I can make out the rounded ears and head of a deer silhouetted on the water. I look up at Mama but she only returns my puzzled glance.

"Why isn't it running?" I whisper.

"I think it might be stuck," Mama breathes.

As we edge closer, I can see Mama is right. A young deer lies at an awkward angle, hindquarters high in the air, face and neck pressed against the mud, head turned out to sea. I don't see any spots on the head where antlers would have fallen. She must be a young doe. With my next step, I slip on a rock and lean on Mama. Suddenly aware of our presence, the doe strains every muscle, trying to run. The mud pulls her further in and will not let go.

The water is just around her ankles. She slumps. Her sides move in and out with her breath.

I crouch down, as if somehow my being here is all that is keeping her from freeing herself. Mama kneels beside me.

"How do you think she got down here?" I whisper.

Mama shakes her head. "I don't know. She was probably looking for kelp on the beach and came down too far. She's stuck now though."

The doe strains again, throwing her head back, sending tiny ripples out in the water. Her white throat flashes in the moonlight.

Her head shakes with effort.

"Is there anything that we can do to help her?"

"No sweetie, there's nothing that we can do but leave her be." Mama stands and I push myself up after her. As we start to walk back up towards the cabin, I turn. The doe has moved her neck so that she is looking back at us. Her eyes are wild. I turn away and follow Mama but I can still feel her eyes at my back.

When we reach the basket, I look back one more time. The doe is too far away to really see. But something else is moving towards her.

Her fawn.

Without thinking, I turn back down the beach. Mama follows behind me. When we are halfway there, she touches my back. I stop.

The tide is up to the doe's throat. She has to hold her head up to keep it out of the water. The ripples around her flash as she struggles. The fawn bleats.

The doe's nose drops below the water. She throws her head back up, sending out another ring of ripples. The fawn bleats louder. She turns her head towards her baby, but she's facing the wrong way. Her head slumps beneath the surface, and with it her whole body. The water is still.

Mama puts her arm on my shoulder. I curl against her.

"Let's head back, sweetie."

I dip my head into a nod. She guides me back to the path, with her hand on my back. I can hear the fawn calling out over the water. Calling to the place where its Mama has disappeared.

🌱

Mama shakes my shoulder. I roll over and pull the bed skins over my head. She rubs my back. "Come on, sleepy head," she says. I sit up.

No light comes through the boards over the windows. I rub my eyes. Mama doesn't have water on the stove for tea. I pick up the skin that we use under our heads and wrap it around me on the outside of the other blankets. "It's so early."

Mama nods. "I know, sweetie. But the tide's going out. And we have to get the doe."

Last night floods back. The eyes of the doe, the bleat of her fawn. I imagine the fawn, spending the night alone, backing away from the rising tide.

"What do you think will happen to her fawn?"

Mama takes her coat from where it is drying by the fire. "I'm not sure. It won't be nursing anymore, that's for sure. It probably isn't that much worse off now than it was with its Mama. It should be okay as long as the snow doesn't stick around too long."

I nod but turn my head away. I've seen so many dead deer in the snares that I hardly even think about it anymore. But somehow this is different.

Mama strokes my hair over my shoulders and kisses the back of my head. "Time to get dressed. The tide doesn't wait."

Mama's said 'the tide doesn't wait' at least a thousand times before, when we need to dig clams or when we need to walk around the reef at low tide. I used to say it to Mama when I was little and wanted her to do something. But now I finally know what it means.

The tide doesn't care the doe was in its way last night. The tide doesn't care when Samuel is rowing as hard as he can and can't make headway against the flood. No matter what you do, the tide will always come in, always go out. No matter what is in its path or what it will leave dry.

Mama stands.

"Ready?"

I nod and push myself out of bed. My clothes are hanging by the hearth, stiff with clay from digging clams last night. Mama picks up our deer-dragging rope and coils it around her arm. She slips it over her shoulder and then puts on her boots.

"I'll meet you out by the shed, okay? We'll need to haul some of the old boards so we can get through the mud out to the doe."

"Okay."

She steps out the door. It squeaks as she closes it behind her.

I shiver. We are low enough on wood that Mama didn't even start the fire. I shake the mud off my wool coat and pull it on. The fawn is probably alone in the snow now. Without his Mama.

The tide doesn't wait.

I slip on my boots and open the door. There isn't any light other than the moon, which is just a tiny slice of silver just at the tops of the trees. I follow Mama's footsteps to the beach.

I catch up with Mama at the edge of the trail. She drags a board under each arm. I take one from her and we start to pull them along the snow bank. At the edge of the trees, a tiny patch of snow is melted down to the rye grass. All around it are the fawn's tracks, smaller than the distance between my first and second knuckle.

I set my board down and kneel to get a closer look. Mama stops and looks over my shoulder.

"Poor little guy," she says.

I look at the tracks. The feet sink in so deep, the snow must have been almost up to his belly. "How can he make it in all this snow, Mama?"

"We'll just have to see," she says. "But the tide's dropping, sweetie, we have to go."

FIVE

"The fawn hasn't even moved for days, Mama! How do you expect him to eat?"

Mama doesn't turn around, just keeps her eyes on the soup as she stirs it. We are making real soup for the first time in weeks, now that we finally have meat. Even though it's been cold, it's early enough in the winter that the doe still had plenty of fat. The rich, fatty smell fills the cabin.

"Sweetie, we can't afford to give it our food. Fawns don't make it through the winter all the time, even with their mothers."

"But we killed... She's..." I stop. I know Mama won't listen. I've asked about feeding the fawn ever since we found his bed three days ago. I scrape the knife along a leg bone and flick the last flecks of meat into the soup.

Mama looks up at me. "I know this is hard, but we have to survive, too. Anyway, what do we have that a deer would eat?"

I turn away and talk to the kindling box. "We have rice. Sugar."

Mama stirs the soup, then picks out a chunk of potato and bites it to see if it is cooked through. It crunches. She throws it back in the pot. "I never thought you'd share your sugar, Wild Child," she says. "The answer is still no. The fawn can survive on his own."

I bite my tongue. He can't survive on his own. He can't even move. He'll freeze.

Mama turns away from the stove and strokes my hair. I keep my head as still as I can and stare straight ahead.

"Sweetie, there's nothing else we can do."

I turn from Mama's hand, grab the soup spoon, and start stirring. Mama keeps talking to the back of my head, but I hunch my shoulders and stare at the swirling broth. While we eat our soup, the only sound is the wind outside the cabin.

❧

When I dump the clam shells at low tide the next morning, the air feels a little warmer. I see the spoon-sized tracks in the middle of our trail compacted on top of the snow. I follow them back to where they turn off the path. Where the snow is thinner under a big spruce, I see the dark lump of the fawn's body.

I glance back towards the cabin. Mama won't notice if I'm gone just a little longer. I set the bucket on the path and approach the fawn. His back is to me. Only when I step on a stick does he turn around. I freeze. His brown eyes stare straight back at me.

He jumps away, but he only makes it a few steps before the snow stops him. He turns back around, snow up to his belly.

"I'll get you something to eat, little guy," I whisper under my breath. The fawn keeps staring. I back away slowly.

I reach the edge of the snow and pick up the empty bucket. I can still see the fawn watching me from his place in the snow. He looks so small. "I'll be back," I say to him. "I promise."

"What took you so long?" Mama asks, when I come in.

I shrug. "The snow is deep. It takes a while to make it all the way out there."

"True enough," Mama says. She is stirring the soup from last night with one hand and with the other she adds herbs to the tea water. The smell of the warm food wafts towards me. The kindling box is full, even though I forgot to fill it last night.

I set my boots in the corner then take the soup spoon from Mama.

"Thanks."

She smiles.

The soup is thick, full of meat, potatoes, leftover clams, and even a little rice. With meat now, we have enough. Mama might not even notice a few missing handfuls of sugar.

❧

Without my gloves on, my hands shake so much that I almost spill the sugar. It has finally stopped snowing, but it has gotten so cold that each morning the cracks between the boards in the cabin are coated in a white lace of ice. Whenever I'm cold inside, though, I think about how much colder the fawn must be out in the snow.

I rest my elbows on my knees to wait. Finally the fawn steps from behind a tree. He sees me and moves closer, sniffing the air. For the last week he has let me get close enough to see the nubs of antlers that mark him as a buck, but never close enough to touch him.

"C'mon little guy," I coax. "It's all right, it's just me. Eve."

Slowly, he lifts his leg out of the snow and takes one more step.

"C'mon little guy," I say again.

For the last three weeks I've fed the fawn. At first I would just leave sugar on my mitten at the base of the tree. In the morning the only way I could tell that the sugar had been there were the sticky patches on the red wool. Soon the fawn would come back and start to eat even before I got a chance to walk away. Then he let me sit only a pace away. Whenever I reached out to touch him, though, he would bound away.

The fawn lifts his head and turns his ears towards the cabin. I glance over my shoulder. The cabin door is still closed. Mama's inside.

I turn back. The fawn is so close his breath comes in little warm puffs on my fingers. He looks up at me, then lowers his nose and licks the sugar off my palm. His tongue tickles my fingertips.

I force my hands to stay still. The fawn nuzzles his nose into my hand, licking the sugar from the creases in my cupped palm. His tongue is rough.

Slowly I take one hand from underneath the other and touch the fawn's forehead. The black velvet hair is softer than anything I've ever felt before. He doesn't seem to notice.

🌾

"What about rice pudding tonight?" Mama asks.

I stop polishing the smooth wood of Samuel's fiddle, laying the worn cloth across the strings. Mama only makes rice pudding a few times all winter. And usually only when we have enough other food. Rice pudding is almost as good as the sweet things that Samuel brings us.

I start to nod. We haven't had something sweet since before I started to feed the fawn.

The sugar.

I've almost emptied an entire bag.

"Maybe not tonight, Mama," I blurt.

Mama turns around. "Sweetie, why not?"

"I don't think we should use up the sugar." I take a deep breath. "Let's save some in case Samuel is late this spring." I turn my eyes away from Mama.

"We still have a half a sack left plus a full one we haven't even opened." Mama looks at me the same way she does when I get hurt and won't tell her. "You love rice pudding."

"I...I'm just not very hungry."

Mama stands up and walks over to the bag. "I'm sure you'll want some once it's done." She reaches for the sack. I twist my hands in the deer skin on the bed.

"Eve?" Mama turns, the empty bag rumpled in her hands. "What happened to the sugar?"

I think of the fawn, his scratchy tongue, his brown eyes, his soft forehead.

"Mama, he was going to starve. He hadn't moved for two days. I don't care what you say, he would have died without sugar." I am standing now, facing Mama at the other side of the room. The soup bubbles behind us on the stove. "He waits for me every morning now, Mama," I say, my voice softer. "He eats out of my hand."

Mama smoothes the sugar bag down, turns, and places it in the basket. Slowly she turns back towards me. "Eve. How many times did I tell you no? How many times did I tell you it was a waste of our food?" She sighs and moves back to the soup. "The fawn might have survived before, but now he's dependent on our food. He'll probably die without it."

I take a step towards Mama. The stove is still between us, but I stare her in the eye. "If you drowned, you'd want someone to take care of me."

Mama's face freezes. I keep my eyes glued on hers. She looks down to the floor. Her shoulders rise and fall with a long, shaky breath. Then she grabs her coat from the hook and reaches for her boots.

"I'm going to go outside, Eve." Her voice is mechanical. Before I can say anything the door swings shut behind her.

I stand on the hearth, looking at the closed door. The soup bubbles on the stove next to me.

Mama's never left like that before.

I look down and see my hands clenched in fists. I feel like I am almost about to cry but I stop myself. "There's nothing wrong, Eve," I say aloud. *Mama just went outside.*

The fire pops. I crawl under the bed skins and curl up facing the wall. Part of me wants to wait for Mama. To make sure she comes back. But instead I force myself to fall asleep to the sound of the cooling woodstove in the quiet cabin.

❦

Snow slides off the roof and lands in a muffled thump in the snow bank, waking me up. The fire's going but Mama's not inside. After last night, I don't want to see her. Even if we didn't talk about what happened, it would hang in the air between us. I slip out of the blankets, pull on my coat, and go out the door. I dart behind the cabin, hoping Mama doesn't see me. I sit behind the chopping block and rest my chin in my hands. I don't see the fawn until he's three paces away. His brown eyes stare at me. He steps closer.

"I'm sorry," I whisper.

He leans forward and sniffs my closed hand. He doesn't even hesitate to come closer to me. "I don't have sugar for you." He flicks his tail and looks up. I dig my fingernails into my palm. He steps forward and nuzzles my hand again.

"I'm sorry." My voice cracks, sounding twice as loud as I mean it to. The fawn jumps back.

"It's all right." I try to coax him back, but his tail stays high in alert. He looks at me one last time and then turns into the woods.

I hear Mama's footsteps on the porch. I push myself up and run after the fawn.

I don't pay attention to where my feet are going, just let myself run. I go around the potato patch, and then break out onto the beach. The water is calm. I run over the rocks, as fast as I can go. When I reach the base of the cliffs, I scramble up my path, stopping at the top. The day is gray and dull. I wrap my arm around a tree and rest my cheek on the rough bark, looking back towards the cabin instead of out over the water. The sound of my breath is the only thing in the still woods.

I kick at the snow with my boot. It starts an avalanche of tiny snowballs down the path and then off the cliff into the water.

Mama will be wondering where I am. But I don't care. She was so calm when she talked about the fawn. She doesn't care about him any more than she cares about a handful of sugar. Why should I worry about her worrying?

I pull my arms into my coat and hug myself to stay warm. Sweat from running cools on my back, sucking all the warmth from my skin. I think about the fawn's wet nose. What if Mama is right? What if the fawn will die now? I imagine finding his body stiff and frozen in the snow. What if Mama won't let me feed him? Or what if we just run out of sugar?

There's got to be something else I can feed him. I lean against the tree and press my face into the bark. Why did the doe have to drown? Why did the fawn have to lose his Mama?

I watch the gentle waves move along the curve of the cove, starting just by the reef and arching all the way to the creek. The tide is at its lowest point, just starting to come back in. Maybe I can feed the fawn rice. If I soak it first. And I don't eat too much so that we don't run out. And I can feed him a little less each day so that he learns to find his own food.

I push myself away from the tree and brush the bark out of my hair. All I have to do is feed the fawn until spring. And by next winter he'll be okay on his own. I climb down the path, knocking snowballs in front of me. They roll down and launch off onto the wet rocks, crumbling into slush.

I jump off the last rock, and walk towards the cabin. I don't want to see Mama. Don't want to talk to her. She thinks the fawn is just another deer we should eat.

A seal watches me from just off shore, its round head moving in and out of the water. The fawn would have died without me. I didn't kill him. I saved him. Mama would have let him starve underneath the tree, shivering.

I duck under the spruce branches at the potato patch, and walk toward the cabin inside the trees. If Mama's inside, maybe I can go out and chop wood. Or find any way to stay away from her. Just as I reach the back of the cabin, I see something blue out of the corner of my eye. I stop. It's the blue of Mama's wool coat.

She's kneeling in the snow, with her hand out in front of her. Something moves but a tree blocks my view. I take another step towards her.

The fawn.

Mama is feeding the fawn. After everything she said. I take off through the snow, as fast as I can go without making the fawn bolt. The snow is almost up to my knees, but I feel so light I don't notice. Tiny patches of winter sun sneak through the trees and shine off the snow.

Mama doesn't turn until I'm right behind her. She smiles.

I don't know what to say. But I just smile back. Then we both turn to the fawn.

"It's okay, little one," Mama coaxes. "I won't hurt you."

The fawn looks straight at her but doesn't move. I walk up and put my hand on Mama's shoulder. She turns and looks at me.

"Here," I whisper. "Let me hold it." Mama dumps the sugar into my cupped hands. The fawn comes up and licks greedily. Mama reaches out and strokes his forehead. He doesn't step away.

The fawn's ears swivel towards the beach. His tail flicks. I look at Mama. She doesn't seem to notice.

The fawn lowers his head again, but keeps one ear pointed to the beach.

I hear a shout. It sounds like Uncle Samuel's voice but deeper. Oarlocks clank. My mind races. Today was the first day I didn't check for boats. The first day the water was calm in weeks. I hear it again. This time I can make out the words.

"Spread out! Search!"

Mama's face is white. I reach out to grab her hand, but she has already taken mine and is running. I catch a glimpse of the fawn bolting away. The voices grow louder. Mama veers over towards the stand of alders by the cabin.

"Mama? The ravine? They can find us here."

Mama pushes her way into my hiding spot and pulls me behind her.

"There isn't time, Sweetie," she whispers. "Just don't move. Don't let them see you."

SIX

Mama's back pushes me against the tree. Ridges of the bark dig into my skin. I hear the voices moving closer.

"Had no idea this was all happening under our noses. Shame, too. Samuel was quite a guy."

"He had it coming though. I thought something was going on ever since she escaped. I knew it wasn't a coincidence that she was his sister."

Two men come out of the trees, walking on our path. Through a gap in the branches I can just see their knees. Mama presses me closer to the tree.

"What do they mean?" I whisper in her ear. She presses her hand over my mouth.

"Well," the first man sighs. "It's all taken care of now."

"I just hope we find her and get out of here before night. This sure is a sorry excuse for a shack."

Boots clunk up the cabin steps. So close. Only five paces from us. I take Mama's hand.

They go in the door, without knocking the snow off their boots. Their voices inside are muffled.

There is a thump. Something clatters. "Dammit! You can't see a thing in here."

"The windows are covered, Henry. It's better when your eyes get used to it," calls the second man. "C'mon." One set of boots stomps farther inside. Closer to us.

"Steven, she's obviously not in the cabin. What are you doing?"

Mama sucks in a sharp breath.

"What's going..." I whisper as softly as I can.

"Shhhhhh," she hisses.

More boots clunk to the back of the cabin. The wood stove door squeaks.

"We can at least tell how long it's been since she was here. See, there's still coals in the stove."

Mama's heart pounds against my cheek. Her hand is sweating in mine, still sticky from the sugar.

"Then she can't be far. She's an Imperfect for god's sake, not a superhero."

"She's managed to survive here. For twelve years. She probably knows how to get around."

Melting snow seeps through my skirt. With Mama pressing against me, it feels twice as hard as it should to breathe.

The loose board by the hearth groans from inside the cabin. I can picture the men, one kneeling by the stove, one flopped onto the bed. Picture snow from their boots melting in puddles on the floor.

"Once you've finished your little detective search, let's go out and help the boys. They might need extra hands rounding her up."

"Henry, come off it. The Founding Act said to insure the Imperfects lived in comfort without multiplying and infecting society with their defects. It didn't say anything about herding them up like cattle."

"Just listen to you. You sound like one of those preaching doctors from training. Quoting The Founding Act."

"Can't help it. My father was one of those 'preaching doctors.'" There is a harsh chuckle from the cabin. More footsteps. "Okay, I'm done searching. Let's go help the boys. You go to the east and I'll head up the west side of the valley."

I watch as the boots come down the cabin steps and back towards the beach. I try to crane my neck around to follow where they go, but Mama pushes me back.

"OK, sweetie," she whispers. "Once they're at the beach, we'll run back towards the ravine. At the west valley wall, walk in the creek to the top. I'll make tracks on the other side of the valley. Then come back for you. Just stay out of the snow. It will all be over soon."

I squeeze Mama's hand tighter. "But what if...?"

"We have to go now. Before they see our tracks leading here." She stands, and we duck through the low spruce branches. Mama pulls me along again, gripping so tight that I feel like my hand might break. Blueberry branches sting across my face as I run, making me squint. Suddenly, Mama looks back.

"Walk in my tracks. I don't want them to see where we separate."

I step behind Mama. Our pace slows to almost a walk with me following. Every devil's club, every spruce branch holds us back. Mama's fingernails dig into my palm. Each footstep in the snow sounds loud enough to hear on the other side of the Island.

I hear the crunch of a boot behind us. I swivel my head over my shoulder. The snowy woods are still. Mama tugs forward.

"C'mon, sweetie."

Behind Mama's head, something moves on the valley wall. Another man. He's too high up to be either of the ones in the cabin. He has his back to us but if he turns around, we're in plain sight.

"Mama..." I point up the hill.

She turns her head and stares at the hillside. Her hand clamps onto my shoulder. The man moves out of sight, without looking back. Mama turns and wraps her arms around me.

"I've got to go now, sweetie," she whispers. Her face is streaked with tears.

I cling to her, just like I used to when I had nightmares.

She puts her hands on my shoulders and holds me at arm's length.

"Promise me you won't let any of the men see you. Promise me you'll be okay."

I look back at Mama. I don't know when I started, but I'm crying, too.

"I promise," I whisper.

Mama hugs me again. "I love you," she says. Then she lets me go and steps out of the creek.

"Mama, don't..."

Before I can finish, a stick snaps behind us. The man following our tracks is just around the bend on the creek. Mama shoves me into the snow before he can see me. Then she sprints off the other way.

The man flashes past me. His hat falls into the snow, showing red curls underneath. I push myself up. He grabs Mama's arm. She stumbles and tries to jerk away.

"Sarah," he says. It's the voice of the man who opened the woodstove in the cabin. Steven.

Mama turns back to him and tries to wrench free again.

"Goddamnit, Steven, let me go. We have to get away from here. The others can't see me here."

The man holds tightly to her hand.

"Sarah?" he asks. "Let's go back to the boat. Then we'll have some time—just the two of us."

Mama tries to pull her arm free. The man almost loses his grip. He puts his other hand on her shoulder and tries to turn her towards him.

"Don't worry," he says, "I won't let them hurt you. The society is different now. I promise. Better lodging. Higher quality. I've gotten the Imperfects better care."

Mama's face is suddenly wild. In a way that I haven't ever seen. Her voice is low, but so harsh it sounds like a snarl.

"Oh, so you think you're good enough that I'll want to go back and live in a 'high quality' prison cell just to see you strut around in uniform?"

The man steps backward, still clutching Mama's arm. The snow reaches almost over his shiny boots.

"Sarah, I..."

Mama leans towards him, her eyes narrowed. She's whispering, but so sharply her words slice through the cold air.

"I didn't just run away from your torture chamber because I could. I did it to keep you and your 'high quality society' from killing someone."

Mama points at me.

The man turns. His eyes lock onto me. I'm frozen. Rooted in the snow. The man's eyes are blue. Not the soft brown of Mama's. Or the green of Samuel's.

Mama wrenches her arm free. She takes another step towards the man. "And if they see her here, they'll kill her without a second thought."

The man takes a step towards me. I unfreeze. And run.

I dash upstream in the creek. Out of the corner of my eye I see Mama sprinting the other way. When I reach the log jam, I scramble over the slippery mat of roots and logs then keep going. A layer of ice collects on my boots. As the ravine gets steeper, the rocks are so slippery I can hardly move forward without falling two steps back. My hands are too cold to grab hold of anything.

When I reach the top of the steepest pitch, I stop. My hands are numb with cold, but the rest of me still feels warm. I look down the creek in the snowy woods. There is no sign of anyone.

Mama's scream echoes up the valley. It rings in my ears, long after the air is still again. I listen for something else. Except for the rustling of hemlock needles, there is nothing.

Cold finally starts seeping into me. I step out of the creek into the snow. The ice on top of my boots snaps as I move my ankles.

I'll come back for you. It will all be over soon.

I sit on a snow-covered log and lean against the hemlock behind it. I'll just wait for Mama. My teeth chatter. She'll come back. She said she would. She has to.

But the man already saw Mama. Mama called him Steven. And he saw me. And Mama screamed. They would have heard her. They would have caught her.

But the man already caught her. And walked to me. He called Mama Sarah.

I hug my knees to my chest and press my face into them. I'll just wait for Mama. Just wait for Mama.

The next scream is so far away that I can hardly hear it. It comes from out over the water, and echoes off the cliffs across the valley.

I jump up. The hillside slopes down to the still valley floor. I stand at the top, then sprint down. Every step punches knee-deep into the snow. Avalanches cascade down in front of me. Blueberry bushes snap my face.

At the valley floor, I dash across the creek and stop.

The men's tracks are everywhere.

They crisscross all over the valley floor, past where Mama and I ran to the creek. Down from the valley wall. Up towards the snare trails. I bend down and try to look for the familiar mark of Mama's boots. If I can find her tracks, I can follow where she went. Where she was screaming.

Finally I see the place where Mama pushed me into the creek. The tracks of the man who followed us. Tracks where Mama ran. I follow her footprints, so worn down that I can only see a boot shape, none of the markings of the sole. There is a scuffle, the mark of a body being pushed into the snow. Then all I can see is the sharp marks of the men's boots.

I turn back to the cabin and try to run. The snow is so deep that it is hardly faster than a walk. The men's tracks are bunched together now, all going in the same direction. One set leads right up to my hiding spot, where Mama and I were. But the marks of Mama's boots are gone.

I run to the beach. There is a deep groove in the sand from the hull of a boat. The rising tide laps at it, eating away at the mark. One of Mama's mittens floats at the water's edge.

There is no sign of a boat in the strait.

I look down at my own boots, caked in snow. Mama's mitten floats between them, the ragged end of the wrist where she took off yarn to patch my mittens drifts in the water. The only sound is the gentle slap slap of the water on the beach.

Something wells up inside of me. I take off sprinting. Down the beach. Over the rocks. Stumbling on the seaweed between the snow and the incoming tide.

Once I reach the rocks I dash up the path. My boots slip and my knee jams into the jagged bedrock. A patch of blood stains my pants but I don't feel anything. I push myself up and scramble to the top of the cliffs. The water is perfectly calm. So far that I have to squint to see it, the boat slides across the calm water. The rhythmic motion of the oars makes a splash of glistening white, in and out, in and out. Each stroke pulls them further away.

A drop of blood runs down my leg. The only sound in the woods seems to be my breath.

"Mama!" I scream. My voice shatters the still air.

"Mama!"

The only reply is the echo from the mountain.

SEVEN

I shiver.

Cold hearth stones. Wood floor. Icy air. Black night. They suck all the warmth out of my body. Pressing me down, flattening me. Cold worms its way under my tunic, under my hair, into my bones.

I close my eyes against the blackness. And keep them shut against the tears leaking out underneath.

When I wake again, sun peaks through the cracks of the boards over the windows. I lift my face from the floor. My neck aches. My shoulder pinches where it has pressed into the corner of the hearth.

Why is it so cold?

Mama didn't start the fire.

Where is she?

I push myself off the floor. Pain shoots up my leg when the cut on my knee rubs on the boards. And with it comes the memory of yesterday. The cliffs. The boat.

Mama's scream.

I remember walking back to the cabin in the dark. Tripping on the steps and crawling to the hearth. Crying on the floor, without even trying to climb into bed.

I sink back down, this time with my head and arms resting on the bed skins. I hear Mama's scream over and over. And its faint echo off the mountain, far off and soft like the last call of cranes when I'm not sure if I hear them or not.

I press my hands over my ears to try to block it out, but it still rings. I lift my head and look around the cabin. The tea cups are sideways on the floor, and the bed skins are knotted. The wood stove door hangs open.

I jump up and slam it shut. The metal clangs in the frozen air, then the hinges swing open again. This is all because of the men. The man who followed us. Who looked at me.

I push the image of him away. I can't think about him now. I grab the pot from the stove. I'll make tea. Just like Mama would.

I dip the pot into the water bucket. It clinks against the solid ice at the bottom.

I let the water freeze.

I'll just have to go to the creek. I do it all the time. I pick up the bucket and open the cabin door. Peachy morning light streams onto my face. I picture Mama by the creek, the sun on her long brown hair. If she were there, we would carry the water bucket back to the cabin together. A cabin warm from Mama's fire.

I hug my coat tighter around my shoulders. I still have all my clothes on from yesterday, but it feels cold enough for them to be made of paper. I look at the patch on the thumb of my mitten, where the blue fabric is tightly stitched with the red yarn. The yarn that Mama unraveled from the wrist of her own mitten.

Her mitten. It was floating by the boat. I set the empty water bucket down. The metal handle makes a dull clank on the hard plastic, but I'm already running down the porch steps and out to the beach. I stumble over my stiff legs, almost falling in the snow.

The tide is halfway out. Crystals of slushy saltwater ice coat the rocks, shining pink in the morning sun. I step off the snow bank. The men's footprints are still there, frozen in the sand. A few paces away is the groove from the hull of the boat. I don't see the mitten.

A lump rises in my mouth. I swallow it down. The mitten shouldn't have gone far. I walk the shore, towards the mouth of the creek. Gentle waves lap against the edge of the gravel. Sun sparkling off the snow hurts my eyes.

Just at the mouth of the creek, a patch of bright red flashes against the sand. I run and pull the mitten from the kelp line. It is covered in sand and seaweed, and frozen in a cup shape. When I pull the seaweed off, a tatter of yarn comes with it.

Slowly I walk back up the beach, holding the mitten against my chest. I don't tell my legs to move, they just carry me. When I get to the porch, I don't go up the steps but alongside the cabin wall. Without thinking, I duck into my hiding spot. Where Mama pressed me into the tree, I can see the simple marks of her boots. I stare at them, imagine Mama's shoes were there. Imagine Mama's feet filling those shoes. Imagine Mama filling the space in front of me. Her smell filling my nose. I remember how hard I squeezed her hand before we ran.

I sink down onto my root, wincing as my knee bends. The snow's cold seeps into me, but it doesn't feel sharp like it should. Like someone else is feeling the cold and I am just imagining it. I'm not Eve down there under the tree. I'm just pretending to be.

Something pushes my elbow.

I turn. The fawn nuzzles his nose in my armpit. It should tickle, it should make me laugh, but it just feels dull like the cold. I can't feel. I can't laugh. I push his head away. He sniffs Mama's mitten in my hand and looks up at me.

"I can't feed you!" My words are louder than I mean them to sound. I stare at him. If he hadn't made me feed him, Mama wouldn't have fed him, either. She wouldn't have been so close to the beach. We could have run straight to the ravine.

"This is all your fault!" I shout. "You greedy little thing, you greedy little deer." I stand and push him away. My hands are shaking.

The fawn backs away into the bushes. His brown eyes look straight up at me. I run at him.

"Go away."

He stares at me.

"Didn't you hear what I said? GO AWAY!"

The fawn sprints away, then stops and looks over his shoulder. I throw Mama's mitten at him. It sticks in the spruce branches and then falls out of sight.

"Find your own sugar," I yell. "I can't take care of a deer who eats people's food. I am a human. I should be trying to eat you."

He leaps across the creek and disappears down the path toward the snares.

"Good," I call after him. "I'm glad you finally went back to where you belong."

I turn and walk toward the cabin. Tears push on my eyelids. I blink them back. "Stupid fawn. There's no point in crying for him."

I open the cabin door. The air inside is just as cold as it is out. The bed is still unmade. I should start a fire. I curl up under the bed skins. I should go back out and get water for tea. My tears flow onto the fur.

"Stupid fawn."

❧

The darkness pushes on my eyes. I can feel tightness on my cheeks where tears dried. The pillow is damp against my neck. The air is so cold it hurts to breathe. The bed skins are as frigid as a snow bank, the cabin as icy as a winter night. I can just barely see the outline of the wood stove lurking by the bed.

I've never been alone in the dark without Mama.

I slide out of bed and put my feet on the floor. I didn't even take my shoes off before I got into bed. I take a step. My foot slams into the hearth. I catch myself on the woodstove, knocking the pot to the floor. The lid rolls across the boards then clangs in circles until it finally vibrates to a stop. My foot squishes into something cold and wet. I kneel down in the slop.

Potatoes! Mama must have put them on the stove before she left. I reach down and scoop up a handful. I didn't know I was hungry. Now I'm starving. The bigger chunks are hard and barely cooked, encased in ice crystals. I take a bite. The cold makes my teeth ache. The sharp bitter taste of a spruce needle explodes in my mouth. I swallow and take another mouthful.

The old Eve never would have done this. The old Eve would have started a fire, would have cooked the potatoes, would have taken care of herself.

I scrape the last of the potatoes out of the cracks in the floorboards. My hand runs into one of the tea cups on the floor. I should be able to control myself. The dirt mixed in with the potatoes makes me cough.

I walk outside. Eerie beams of moonlight snake out of the clouds and through the branches. I duck behind the spruce trees and walk towards my hiding spot, keeping a hand on the wall of the cabin to guide me. The wind has come up and spruce needles scratch across the roof.

At the edge of the cabin, I kneel and start to crawl. It is almost pitch-black underneath the trees. There's no way to see the mitten.

But it should be here. Where I threw it towards the fawn. I crawl farther from the cabin wall. The hard crust on the frozen snow scratches my wrists. Trees block the way, grabbing at my hair. The fawn. It wasn't his fault. It was all mine. I was mad at Mama. I wasn't fast enough when we ran. I didn't come to her when she screamed. I cough. Snow showers down from the branches above.

I think of Samuel hunched over in the waves, riding the storm. Of Mama's scream when she got caught. It's all my fault. I chased the fawn away. I made Samuel go into the storm. He was worried about me getting caught. Mama... My stomach cramps. I vomit, hurling the potatoes back out into the snow. They took Mama because of me. Because Mama didn't want them to see me. I gag, and vomit again. If I hadn't gotten so mad, we could have gone to the ravine together, the man wouldn't have found us. I turn towards the cabin, but all there is in front of me is trees and blackness.

"I'm sorry, Mama," I whisper. I lean my face against an alder, sending snow falling down on my neck.

"I'm sorry."

EIGHT

I lean all my weight into the shovel and push the pile of snow off the porch. Eve liked snow. She was happy when it started to fall. She liked it when the piles got so high she could climb up the snow bank onto the roof. I look out at the relentlessly falling snowflakes. Cold. Wet. Grey. For five days straight now.

I don't like the snow anymore.

I push another shovel load off. The snow bank swallows it with a dull thump. It's been two weeks since they took Mama. Silence hangs in the grey air. Two weeks since I've seen the fawn. I press the edge of the shovel into a crack between the porch boards and lean into the handle. The metal is cold on my collar bone. I stare at the flurry of snowflakes against the dark trees. I'm always like this without Mama. Stopping. Staring. No jokes. No laughing.

Finally I pry the metal edge from its space between the boards and start working again. The shovel catches on a stick wedged between two boards. Snow scatters everywhere. I wince as the handle jams into my stomach.

This same thing happened the day before they took Mama. We were shoveling together when the edge of Mama's shovel caught. She flew into the snow bank, arms pinwheeling. I tried to shovel more snow on top of her, but I snagged the same stick and flew the other direction. We sat there, buried in snow, laughing until our sides hurt. Finally Mama pulled me up and we brushed the snow off each other where it clung to our wool coats. I went inside and started making tea while Mama finished shoveling. I could hear her singing until the excited rattle of the boiling water drowned out her voice.

I rip the stick out from the boards and throw it hard. It slams into the side of the cabin, then plops in the snow.

"It's just a stupid stick!" I shout.

There's nothing to worry about. Nothing to cry about.

I wipe my nose on the shoulder of my coat, and start pushing the shovel. The slush is so deep, it takes all my body weight to make any progress at all. The shovel squeaks and groans across the boards. The fawn used to stand on the side of the house while I shoveled, waiting for food. Sometimes he'd stand so close that I would dump a load on top of him, and he'd stot off into the woods to shake it off. It was never long before he'd come back.

I smile then sigh. The only mark in the snow now is where the stick disappeared. The pile is so deep now that the fawn wouldn't have to climb onto the porch, he'd just step from the snow. The memory seems so far away. It wasn't though. Two weeks.

But I haven't seen any sign of the fawn since I chased him. His tracks were completely covered by snow that night. He ran right down the path to the snares. The snares. I can't bring myself to check them.

I've only seen one set of deer tracks by the cabin since. I don't know if they are the fawn's.

I lean the shovel against the siding. It squeaks as the metal slides across the porch. I look out to where I saw the tracks. They've been buried by snow for three days, but I still remember exactly where they were.

I stomp the snow off my boots and step into the cabin. If those tracks were the fawn's, he's still too afraid to let me see him. And if they weren't his, where is he? I close the door softly so the fire doesn't puff. I don't want to imagine it.

I look at the tea pot. Mama would make tea. The old Eve would have gone out to refill the water bucket. I lift the pot from the stove. Mama and I would have laughed together as we warmed up. We might even have meat from the snares.

To make tea I'd have to go back out to the creek. And haul the water bucket all the way back. I set the pot back on the stove. Then I'd have to stoke the fire. Then I'd have to actually make tea.

I crawl under the bed skins and curl up as small as I can go.

When I wake, sun peeks through the chinks in the boards over the windows. I blink and stare at it. Dust swirls in the thin beams of light. I rub my eyes. It's brighter than it has been for weeks. I push off the skins and run outside in just my socks. The clouds are gone. Pale blue sky shows over the trees. The snow has stopped.

Sunlight sparkles on each snowflake. The old Eve would have loved this. Now it's too much. The light makes me want to cover my eyes, not run out into it. The snow looks icy and wet. I turn back to the cabin.

As I turn to shut the door, I see the fawn. He's walking to the cabin in my newly shoveled path, ears pointed at me, just like he used to do. He licks his nose and sniffs. The sun glints off the snow around him.

I run towards him.

He walks backwards, stuck in my tracks. Still afraid.

I kneel down. The fawn steps closer. "It's okay, little guy," I whisper. "It's okay." He reaches his nose out, sniffing for sugar.

"I don't have anything for you, little one." I can see his ribs through his fur. I reach out to pet his head. He backs away.

"I'll go get some sugar."

He stares at me. I walk backward to the cabin so I can watch the fawn. He sniffs the air but doesn't move.

My socks are soaked. Cold creeps in-between my toes. If I feed him maybe he'll forgive me.

Before I step in the door, I look back one more time. He seems so small and alone in the snow. If only I could warm him up. If only I could bring him inside.

The fawn lifts his head, and licks his nose to sniff. He's so little. It would be easy to pick him up, easy to carry him. We could curl up by the fire. We could sleep in the same bed.

I walk back down the stairs. "Come on little guy," I whisper.

He takes a step. I stand and wrap my arms around his waist. He kicks, arching his back, knocking his head into my chin. My teeth bite into my lower lip. I try to reach down to keep his legs under him but they're flailing around.

"It's all right. It's all right. I'm not going to hurt you."

I bend my legs and support the weight of his chest with my knees. I can feel his heart pounding. Pounding like a hammer on the inside of his ribs. I pull his legs under him, pin them to his belly with my arm. "It's all right," I say into his ear. "We'll just go up the steps. You'll be okay."

I make it across the door frame and set him down by the woodstove. His hoofs slide on the hard floor.

"See, we're all right." But I don't sound very convincing. I hold out my hands. He stares at me. Then turns and runs, knocking me backwards. There is a sickening crunch as my hand slams into Samuel's fiddle. The fawn stumbles down the steps and onto my path then stots off into the trees. The last thing I see is his tail held high in alarm. The floor is left with the zigzagging wet marks from his hoofs.

I lift my hand from the crushed instrument. The bridge is snapped in half, strings hanging sideways. A jagged crack runs from just underneath the neck out towards the edge. The sugar that flew from my fist is scattered on the floor, some of it dissolving in the water that drips from my socks. The cabin is just as cold as outside, the door has been open for so long. I've broken the fiddle. That I promised to take such good care of. I've lost the fawn. Again.

I close the door and walk back to the bed. What smelled so good in the fall is now the stench of musky baskets and stale food. The rafters where the salmon fillets used to be glower at me in emptiness. Just above the stove, the only berry cakes left are the three cranberry ones which were too sour to eat.

In the other corner, the sacks of food from Samuel are a small pile of crumpled bags. There's half a sack of salt and a nearly-empty bag of rice. The bag of sugar with just a few cups left in the bottom. I look at Mama's coat that I left on the floor. I can just hear her say—

Eve, pick that coat up! Sometimes you really are a wild child.

I turn my back to the coat. As though I want to hide my tears from it.

I walk over to the corner and scrape a handful of sugar out of the bottom of the bag. Why didn't I just give the fawn a little? He's hungrier than I am. I pour the sugar from one hand to the other. It's too late. He's gone, too.

Something crashes on the porch. I almost drop the sugar.

The men. They're coming back for me. I haven't checked for boats since Mama left. The wind has been calm. I flatten myself against the wall behind our empty berry basket. Their feet skitter on the boards. There is a soft *womph* like something landing in the snow. Then quiet.

I stand and walk slowly to the door, lift the latch as quietly as I can and peer out. The shovel is knocked over, but I don't see anything else. I push the door open and step out. The fawn stands in the snow bank, up to his chest.

He came to the door. He came! I want to run and hug him but that would only scare him. I kneel down and hold out the sugar still clenched in my fist.

The fawn sniffs but won't come closer. I walk on my knees to the edge of the porch and hold out my hand. He touches his soft, wet nose to my fingers. I don't move.

He steps forward and licks the sugar from my palm. When the sugar is half gone, I close my fingers around it. He nudges my knuckles. I scoot backwards and open my hand. The fawn stares at me, then puts his front feet onto the porch, one at a time.

"Come on, little guy. It'll be warm in the cabin. We'll figure out something you can eat." He takes a step closer. I let him have another lick and then back all the way over inside the door. He stretches his head over the door frame. Gently he puts his front legs on the wood floor. His hoofs slide.

"You'll get used to it. It's warm in here."

He puts his other foot in. Then both his back legs. I open my hand all the way, let him have all the sugar he wants.

The cabin doesn't feel empty anymore. The berry drying racks that I made with Mama are propped neatly in the corner. The rye-grass braids that I braided by myself last summer drape from the ceiling. The potato buckets I filled when Mama's back was hurting wait for the next harvest. The wood box is full of kindling I chopped this morning. I turn back to the fawn.

He licks up the last bit of sugar then pushes his tongue into the creases in my palm. It tickles. I giggle.

The laugh feels funny in my throat. It makes me laugh harder. The sound fills the cabin. It's startling, surprising, and somehow funny. The laughter dances out of my mouth and drifts through the food baskets. It rises over the rafters where the salmon fillets used to hang. It flows out the door and into the empty woodshed. It fills the whole valley, like Samuel's music. It goes over the ridge to whatever is on the other side, to inland and cranes, to Samuel and Mama.

I'm laughing.

I'm ticklish.

I'm Eve.

The fawn stops licking and looks at me. I stroke the top of his head.

"We're both going to be all right, little guy."

The fawn just stands looking at me, the sun streaming into the cabin behind him. He flicks his tail. Maybe tomorrow I'll go check the snares.

NINE

I slide the knife across the stone in long, slow strokes. I can remember the feeling of Mama's fingers over mine, remember her telling me how to hold the knife at the right angle, how to keep from wearing down the edge. I touch the blade to my thumb. Not nearly sharp enough. The stove crackles behind me. I slide the vent closed till only a sliver of orange light shines through, keeping it from eating through the wood too fast.

I focus on the knife again. Ten strokes one way, ten strokes the other way. I test the blade on my thumb, then scrape it backward up my arm. It doesn't cut the hairs. I touch it to my thumb again. I've sharpened the knife plenty of times before. I can do this.

I need to do this. There was barely any food left when they took Mama. And I've saved all the sugar for the fawn since he came back. For the past few weeks I've only let myself have a little rice, and part of a potato each day. The tide won't be low enough for clams again for a few weeks. I can't make it much longer without meat.

Ten strokes on one side, ten strokes on the other. The *shwip shwip* of metal on stone falls into a rhythm. I test the blade on my arm. Fine shiny hairs collect on the edge. I slide the knife into its leather sheath and drop it into my skirt pocket. What else do I need? One of the last salmon fillets is on the hearth, half eaten. I should save it. Hunger twists at my stomach. I snatch it up and drop it in my pocket too. After one last look around I pull on my boots and step out the door.

I slog through snow towards the meat cache. The fawn bumps his head into the back of my leg, making me jump. I smile. He snuck up on me from where he slept in the woodshed, staying in my tracks where I've compacted the snow. I reach down and touch his forehead, then turn back to the meat cache. I take the pack frame from its hook and slide it onto my shoulders. The sky is clear, the snow heavy and soft on the ground. Getting to the snares will take forever. But I don't have a choice. The only thing that breaks the quiet is the soft squeak of my feet.

The fawn follows me into the woods. Then he stops, snow up to his belly, watching me walk away.

"It's okay," I coax. "Just follow in my tracks, the snow isn't too bad."

He cocks his head to the side, then turns back towards the cabin, stepping in each of my footprints. I start to call after him, then stop. He shouldn't be coming to the snares. I shouldn't have brought him even this far.

I keep going. There is no mark of the trail in the snow, but I remember each turn by heart. I push through the patch of blueberry just before the first snare.

Snow is piled high on the snare log, untouched. The moss around the wire is frozen solid. Undisturbed. No tracks. Nothing. Stillness settles in the woods like a thicker layer of snow. I stand there, staring at the empty snare.

If all the snares are empty... I push the heel of my hand into the empty gnawing hunger in my stomach. No. There still are two left to check. Two more places I could have meat.

I step over the log and follow the trail between the creek and the west knob on the valley floor. Usually, the trail here has the most sign. But I don't see so much as a frozen track. I think of the empty meat cache.

The pack frame catches on a branch above me and I almost lose my balance. Right where my feet slip a set of fresh tracks merges onto the trail. I untangle the frame and kneel down to study their size. A good-sized doe, maybe a small buck headed right for the snare! I walk faster. The knife in my pocket bounces against my thigh.

As soon as I round the corner my heart sinks. The tracks bunch together before the deer jumped over the log and landed safely on the other side. The grass loop is broken, leaving the snare wire sagging on the snow. I squat down and pick up the loose grass strands. It seems like such a long time since I was here with Mama. I remember sitting in the same spot as she taught me how to braid the grass for the first time. I can still hear her voice, still see her kneeling in front of me.

You've got to be patient, little bear cub. Hold the grass in your mouth and braid it tightly.

I hold the grass in my teeth and start braiding. The worn strands break between my teeth and fall into my lap. I spit the loose ends out then pick up the grass again. It's almost too short already. If I bite it one more time, it will be useless.

Careful, wild child. Pinch the grass between your lips to keep it from breaking.

I try again. It holds.

I lift the wire, loop the grass through, and tie it fast to the log. Slowly, I lift my hands. Everything holds.

The woods are silent. A raven calls. I stare at the snare for what feels like a long time. Then I pick up the pack frame again and keep going.

I turn and follow the trail into the brush, towards the last snare. If there's nothing here, I have to get meat some other way. I might be able to get the sea otters on the reef, if I can run between them and the water when they're hauled out. But I don't know how I could kill them after that. The limpets on the other side of the cliff could be a meal, but not a very big one.

Then I see it. I run the last hundred yards.

The buck is one of the biggest I've ever seen. There's no snow on top of him. He must be freshly caught. He kicked all the way through the snow tearing up clods of moss and dirt. His antlers curve into a graceful fork.

I have meat. To last me a month, or maybe even more. I'll be able to give the fawn my sugar. I'll eat something other than chewy clams. I'll make it that much closer to spring.

I kneel down next to the deer and loosen the snare from his neck. His neck jerks out of the rope and drops to the ground. His glazed eyes stare up at me.

"I'm sorry," I whisper. Mama always held the deer while I untied the knot, then lowered them down gently. I lay my hand on the deep brown fur and lift his head back up. His neck is thick and muscular.

I reach into my pocket, take out the knife, flip the clasp of the sheath open, and slide the blade out. Then I roll the deer onto his back, squat behind him, and push out on his legs with my knees so his soft white belly is exposed. The warmth of the intestines slides into my fingers as I begin to open the body.

I remember gutting the doe with Mama after we pulled the waterlogged body from the mud. How the legs were so stiff one of us had to hold them apart. How the body cavity was steely cold, the tiny scraps of abdominal fat white and hard.

I run my fingers over the soft warm fat of the buck.

I pull the carcass up to a nursery log and prop the chest up, letting the blood drain out through where I cut the rectum. The white underside of the tail soaks up the deep red. When the last drops trickle out, I wedge my hands through the incision and under the sternum and wrestle the body onto a clean patch of snow.

I skin quickly, nicking the dark meat five times. There's no reason to be in a hurry. Mama being gone doesn't change anything. But my hands keep moving faster. When the skin is off I rinse the heart and liver in the creek, the blood swirling away in the current. I put them gently in the body cavity, then cut the carcass in half to carry, sitting on the rib cage and twisting the pelvis to break the backbone.

Tying the deer off to the pack frame is easy. I roll the bottom onto the canvas and lash it on. I usually carried the pack frame when Mama's back was bad. But a deer like this we would carry between us.

It takes all my strength to get the frame upright. I squat in front of it and slide my arms through the straps. It feels like I'm putting on a boulder instead of a backpack. I lean forward. Rough canvas straps cut into my shoulder but the pack doesn't move.

There has to be a way to do this. I put my hands against the log behind me and start to push myself back and forth, back and forth, then lunge forward onto my hands and knees. My arms wobble beneath the weight. I crawl to the stump that the snare rope hangs from. *Once I'm standing, it'll all work out.* I push myself to my knees. The straps pinch the soft skin in my armpit. My thighs burn. My hands cut into the log's bark. Finally my legs straighten.

I lean forward on the log, keeping as much weight off my legs as I can. The cabin isn't that far. I just have to turn around and start walking. That's all there is to it.

One at a time, I take my hands off the log, my legs shaking. I take a step forward. And another. My foot snags on a stick. I teeter back and forth before I come crashing down on my stomach, the meat knocking all the air out of me. I lie with my cheek in the snow, gasping. I try to push myself up. The frame is so heavy I can't move.

I will never make it to the cabin.

If Mama were here, we would put the pack frame on a pole and carry it between us. We'd be home before dark. I would lift the meat into the cache while Mama cooked the heart for dinner. We might celebrate with a few potatoes. Or the last part of the berry cakes.

Finally I slip my arms from the pack frame straps and roll forward, leaving the meat in the wet snow. I can taste the salty blood in my mouth from where I bit my lip when I fell. I can feel tears rolling down my face, but it's too much work to wipe them away. I'm tired of crying, tired of everything going wrong. I'm weak from hunger. It's going to take me four or five loads to move this deer. And I only have a few hours before sunset. I've never moved meat in the dark. Not even with Mama.

"Mama," I whisper into the snow. "What do I do?"

॥

When I reach the cabin with the first load, only two front legs, it is already dusk. It took half an hour to wrestle the pack frame out of the snow, unlash the meat and separate the quarters. And even with half the load, I had to take a break at each snare.

I untie the legs and carry them one at a time up the ladder to the cache. The ropes to hang the quarters are stiff from not being used. It takes twice as long to attach them in the dim light.

When I come out, the fawn is at the bottom of the ladder. I climb down and touch his forehead. He sniffs at my pocket.

"Not now, little guy. I've got to get food for *me*."

I leave him at the corner of the porch and turn back into the woods. The light is almost gone beneath the trees. I can get one more load. Then I'll have half the meat safe. I can get the other half first thing tomorrow.

I step off my shoveled trail into the deep snow, careful not to fill my boots. I'm almost too tired to lift my legs. But I have to keep going. My fingers wriggle into my pocket and pull out the salmon fillet. I have venison now. A lot of it. I can afford to eat just a little. I rest the back of the pack frame on a log and take a bite. It's stale and crumbles like sawdust, but I eat the whole thing in just a few bites.

I run my thumbs under the straps of the pack frame to take them off my skin. If I'm careful, this deer should last almost a month. If I get another batch of clams, that can last me until nettles start in the spring. Then Samuel will come back.

I should start checking for boats again. Not for the men. They won't come back. Except for that one, they don't know about me. And Mama won't tell them. I'll check to see when Samuel comes back. After he helps Mama escape again in a wheelbarrow.

It's so dark I can barely make out the outline of the snare wire of the second snare. But I can tell that the grass is holding. I hum into the darkness.

"You are not afraid of the dark, Eve," I say aloud. I remember Mama's voice. *Just think of it this way,* she'd say. *It's just like the daylight but everything in the woods can't see you.*

"But what if they can smell me?" I would ask.

Everything that can smell you is just as afraid as you would be if you could smell them.

I keep walking towards the last snare. But I don't stop humming, to let anything listening to me in the dark know I'm coming.

I don't realize I am at the last snare until the thick brush grabs at my hair. All the blueberry bushes make it even harder to see. My foot lands on something oozy. I look down. The sweet acidic smell of intestines wafts up to my nose. The deer stomach. My heart beats faster. I take one more step and freeze.

The hide is pulled out from under the carcass, leaving the meat in the snow. Guts are strewn everywhere. The quarters I separated scattered. The rib cage is at my feet, with gaping claw marks. The bear woofs in the bushes only paces away. I open my mouth to scream but nothing comes out.

Move away slowly.

I step backward, through the stomach, through the snow. The bear steps into the clearing, snapping his teeth together. It takes every muscle in my body not to run. Please don't come closer, I beg him. Please don't follow me.

I move as smoothly and quickly as I can. I see the silhouette of the bear, front paws on the rib cage, face turned towards me. I turn the corner and he is out of sight. I keep walking until I am close enough to the creek for it to drown out the sound of my footsteps. I turn. And run.

Devil's club grabs at my hair and clothes. Through the brush, past the mossy snare, past the blueberry patch. The knife bounces in my pocket. The bottom of the pack frame bangs into my lower back. Snow flies up around my boots. I sprint up the steps, wrench open the cabin door and slam it closed.

I'm breathing in ragged gasps. I throw off the pack frame and fumble in the dark for our candles. There are only a few left. My fingers wrap around the fattest one. I shouldn't waste light, but I can't stay in the dark. I grope around the hearth for matches. It feels like the bear could still be right behind me. I find the match box, yank it open, and strike one on the edge of the hearth. The bright orange flame expands along with the match's sharp sulfur smell. I hold it to the candle and watch the wick straighten, a teardrop-shaped flame form on its tip. Light fills the corner.

I shake the match out, and shrink into the corner on the bed, my back pressed against the rough boards on the wall, brandishing the candle in front of me. My heart is beating so hard I can hear it. I can still smell the deer stomach on my boots. The candle flickers, making the shadow from the woodstove bounce on the wall. There is barely any warmth left from the fire this morning.

"Mama?" I whisper into the cold cabin, my voice small and squeaky. Instead of breaking the silence, it only makes it worse, only reminds me that I won't get an answer.

TEN

I stomp through the snow toward the meat cache. The snow packs in my boots and melts around my ankles. I wince as the icy water drips closer to my toes. I reach the cache and climb the ladder. My legs are heavy and tired. I hoist myself onto the platform and crawl through the door. The two front legs of the buck are only bones. I've tried to eat slowly, but after two weeks nearly all the meat is gone.

I push the leg bones out the door. They disappear into the snow. I imagine the path to the snares, imagine trying to trudge through knee-deep snow. I climb down the ladder. So much has changed. It feels like years since I checked the snares. Yet the fear is close, like I just came running back, just heard the bear's teeth snap. He could still be out there, making his own trails over mine, eating the buck. All of my meat.

I dig the bones out of the snow. Anger twinges in my stomach but it doesn't grow. I'm too scared to be mad. I'm too tired to be mad. I lift the bones and flop them over my shoulder. The snow that sticks on them drips down my back. I'm always behind on something, trying to cut wood, or make soup out of two wrinkled potatoes. I'll have to go back to the snares. There's no other way to make it through the winter.

I turn back down the path to the cabin. I'll go tomorrow. When it first gets light so that I have all day to get down the trail and back.

The pack frame leans against the porch. Even though I scrubbed it as hard as I could in the creek, there are still bloodstains on the canvas. What if the bear is still at the snare?

I speed-walk up the steps to the cabin and pull the door shut as quickly as I can. As if the bear were right behind me. Even if I do go back to the snares, they'll all be empty, I tell myself. The deep snow will have pushed all the deer to the beach.

I pull the soup pot out from the corner, fold the bones into it, and hoist it onto the stove. The ankle joint of one leg is forced open. I scrape a little marrow out with the knife and rub it between my fingers. It's perfectly white and still fatty-waxy. Healthy marrow. It should make the soup stock last a while. And I have one last handful of potatoes to stretch it out. I dip water out of the bucket and pour it over the bones until they are halfway covered. I'll have enough food for a few more days.

The fire sputters. I slide the vent open with my toe and keep working on the soup. Slowly the flames cough back to life with the extra air, but the wet wood doesn't put out much heat. Not nearly enough to boil the bones down. I'll have to cut even more wood before dark.

The fawn's hoofs thump on the porch. I set the lid on the soup pot and open the door for him. He nuzzles my knee then sniffs my pocket. I scratch his head. He comes to visit whenever I haven't been outside for a while but mostly whenever he's hungry. I look up at the sky. There's probably a few more hours of daylight left. Just enough time to get lichen for the fawn and cut firewood. I pull Mama's wool coat off the hook by the door and slide it on. The fawn nudges my pocket. I smile.

"I know you're hungry, little guy. We'll go out and get something to eat." I step onto the porch and close the door behind me. The fawn starts down the path to the beach where I've been collecting lichen for him. I haven't been off my paths since it snowed. From the cabin porch, one path goes to the root cellar, one to the outhouse hole, one to the empty woodshed, and one to the cache. I get sick of staying here in this tiny, cold, world, but the snow is so deep it's hard to go anywhere else.

The fawn trots three paces in front of me. He still stays at least that far away except when he's saying hello or when I have food. He comes in the cabin sometimes, but mostly he's outside with me or sleeping in the shed. Now that there's no firewood left there's plenty of room for him. He stops and waits for me on the edge of the trees, then trots forward when I catch up.

The fawn reaches the spruce tree where I've been getting lichen. He smells the air just to make sure that it's still there, then waits for me again, nose in the air. I start to climb, hanging on to the lowest branches that will hold my weight and then scampering up the trunk. The branches grab at my hair. It's getting long again. Part of me wants to cut it, but I know how much Mama will like it long when she comes back.

I balance on my feet and slowly take my hands off to collect lichen. There's not much left in this tree. I'll have to try a different one next time. I pull my knees onto the branch above me and reach out to a strand hanging an arm's length from the trunk. Looking down in-between my feet I can see the fawn watching from the ground. I shove the lichen into my pocket and climb to the next clump.

The lichen dangles out of the branches right above my face. Standing on the branch, I reach as high as I can and yank it down. I roll the stretchy gray green strands into a ball and stuff it into my skirt pocket. It's almost full. I wrap one more strand around my wrist and start climbing down. A rotten branch groans under my foot. I hang on to two lower branches and walk my feet down the trunk until I'm low enough to jump.

When I land I sink almost up to my knees. The fawn sniffs my pocket. I laugh and scratch his head.

"Even after watching me pick all that, you still have to check to make sure that it's there, don't you?"

He scratches his neck and the base of his head with his back hoof, as if to rub off the scratch I gave him. I unwrap the lichen from my wrist and swing it in front of his nose. He takes one end of it with his lips and starts eating. The other end hangs in the snow. I pick up the loose end and wrap it around his nose. He stops chewing, looks at me, then tries to push it off with his tongue. I giggle.

"Too bad I can't eat lichen like you. Then we wouldn't have anything to worry about."

The fawn finally pushes the long strands off his nose and keeps eating.

"All I have left is that soup I made today. From the leg bones. After that's gone I don't know what I'll do. I won't have anything left."

I give the fawn another strand from my pocket. He takes it from my hand this time almost all in one mouthful. I sit on the log I've been working on for firewood and dump the snow out of my boot. Behind me the saw is still stuck in my unfinished cut. It takes me so long to cut through one round by myself, but I have to if I want soup tonight. The woodshed is empty now.

The fawn nudges my thigh. I pull more lichen out of my pocket. He flicks his tail and leans against my knee. The sun shines low through the trees making the snow sparkle. There's still enough light for me to cut a few rounds. Soon the snow will melt. I'll be able to pick nettles. Samuel will be here. He'll tell me everything about Mama, where she is, when she will come back. Or maybe she'll come back with him.

I stand and start to work on the log. Even though I've been using the saw by myself for weeks, it still buckles. I can remember Mama teaching me to cut the wood.

Only pull, no pushing, or the saw will buckle. Like that!

We always laughed when we made a mistake. There was plenty of time to fix it, plenty of wood left in the shed. Now, there's no one on the other side of the log to pull when I'm not supposed to push. I have to run around the log to pull Mama's side, then back to pull mine. The fawn nudges my leg.

"Oh you're ready for more food, are you?" I chuckle. "While I do all the work with firewood?" Suddenly Mama's voice comes rushing into my ears. When I was wrestling with Samuel.

Crazies. You're wrestling while I do all the work.

My voice sounds almost exactly like hers. I'd never thought of that before.

The fawn nudges me again, harder this time.

"I'll feed you soon, little guy. As soon as I'm done with this cut." My arms are already sore, but I've fallen into a rhythm. Soon I'll be finished. I run over to the other side of the log. I can see the fawn now. He stands straight and stiff with his ears pointing towards the shore. I stop the saw mid-stroke.

The waves lap gently against the beach, so softly I can hardly hear them over the rush of the creek. A raven croaks then snaps his beak. The fawn licks his nose then stretches it out to sniff the wind.

"What is it, little guy?" I whisper. He shifts his weight from foot to foot. Something metallic squeaks and then groans. A muffled splash. Then another.

A boat.

A boat! Uncle Samuel, sugar for the fawn, stories, music, laughter!

Mama.

Mama at last! They're here. I take off running. The first step puts me knee deep in the snow. I don't let that slow me down.

"Mama!" I yell. My voice doesn't sound at all like hers now. It doesn't matter. I keep post holing. Mama! Mama! The beach seems so far away. I can hear the oars splashing. Even closer. Mama!

I break out of the trees. Samuel is already easing the bow of the boat into the creek. I throw myself off the snow bank and onto the rocks. I can go so much faster without the snow. I slip on a strand of seaweed, almost falling. Something about the boat looks wrong. It's too big. Samuel's not in the creek channel. I don't see Mama in the stern. Samuel's coat is thick at the shoulders with red string hanging off all around the edges.

Sarah, you know they're always looking for something to do other than sew more frills on their uniforms.

Samuel turns his head toward me. There are shiny buttons up to his chin. No beard. Red hair pokes out from under his cap. Red hair like mine.

This is not Samuel.

This is the man who took Mama.

ELEVEN

My breath rips in and out of my lungs. I crouch in the snow, just behind the tree fringe near the beach. And gasp. And gasp. The man's shout still rings in my ears.

"Stop! Wait!"

He was so close. Almost as close as he was the day they took Mama. When he stared at me with his blue eyes.

I sink my fists into the snow-covered log in front of me, and push off my knees into a squat. The snow has already soaked through my long underwear. My skirt is so wet it sticks to my legs. Today is clear, so tonight will probably be one of the coldest yet.

Why didn't the man chase me when I ran from him? Why didn't he tie me up and take me away? Maybe he just wants me to freeze out here. Or starve.

I shiver. Sweat from running spreads a chill throughout my body. Mama's wool coat is heavy and damp, but it feels as thin as my cotton blouse it's letting so much air through. I will freeze out here.

I pull my arms inside my coat and my tunic. My fingers run over the ball of lichen in my skirt pocket.

It's spongy under my fingers, still alive and green. Somehow it was only minutes ago that I was feeding the fawn. Only minutes ago that I was cutting wood. Making soup.

The last rays of sun strike the edge of the beach. The woods are already shadowed. I curl my toes in my boots. A pale outline of the almost full moon hangs just above the point. Growing tides. Waves lap gently at the rocks. Soon the water will be right up to the snow bank. Soon the only way back to the cabin will be through the woods. And the deep snow.

I pull the lichen out of my pocket and press it against my cheek. It's rough on my skin. My teeth chatter.

Don't ever let them see you, Eve!

I'll stay here until he leaves. He won't see me. I settle back into the snow and hug myself against the cold. I wish the fawn were here.

I look over the strait. The sun is just a glow along the top of the ridge. As soon as it disappears, the woods will be completely dark. I peer into the trees where I know the path should be. It's just a dark spot among the spruce branches. I can't see the boat in the dark, but I haven't seen it leave. He's still here.

But if he hasn't gone now...he'll have to leave in the dark. I remember the voices of the men, the day they took Mama.

I just hope we find her and get out of this place before dark. It sure is a sorry excuse for a shack.

Maybe, somehow, I missed the boat leaving, maybe I should go back now. But the man could be anywhere. Mama's voice flashes through my head again.

I won't let him see me.

A ray of sunlight strikes the trees. It bobs down the path. But the sun already sank behind the ridge. The light moves closer. I stare through the dead alders. It's an upside-down candle. Bigger than I've ever seen.

It's the man.

He stops on the edge of the snow bank. Has a bundle of something under his arm, and holds the candle up above his head. I can see his face in the whitish light. He has a sharp pointy chin and a biggish nose. Part of me wants to run farther away. Part of me wants to pick up a rock and hurl it at him. To throw his body into the snow and stomp on him. I hate him. I hate that face.

He curls his hand around his mouth and yells into the woods. "Where are you? Come on out." His voice is raspy. Higher than Uncle Samuel's. Something about it reminds me of the baby crows on the beach.

"I won't hurt you. Please, come back out. Please. I brought a blanket." He pauses. "And I've made dinner for us at the cabin."

Dinner? I scrunch the ball of lichen in my hand. He'll kill me.

I won't let you see me! I shout back in my head. *You can't trick me.*

"Please. I know you're here somewhere." He steps off the snow bank. "Can you hear me? Hello? Can you hear me?"

He walks down the beach, between the water and the snow. If he keeps coming, he'll walk right past me. If I move now, he'll hear me. I shrink back into the trees as far as I can.

He stops suddenly and looks around. The blanket rolled underneath his arm is grey and looks soft. He's close enough that I can see the creases at the corners of his eyes. The light shines off the goldish-brown buttons of his coat. He's not shouting anymore, just talking. I can barely hear him.

"Listen, I'm..." He mumbles something I can't hear. "I won't hurt you. I won't take you away."

He comes even closer. My heart pounds. The circle of light from the enormous candle sways back and forth as he walks. I squeeze my eyes shut. I can't let him find me. I have to keep my promise this time.

I see the light pass over my face through my closed eyes. It moves away. I turn my head slowly, careful not to make any sound. The man walks past. The light disappears around the point. I push myself up.

As long as he keeps going just a little farther out, I'll have time to get back to the cabin.

The branches grab at my hair as I scramble out of my hiding spot. My legs are stiff from squatting in the snow. I stumble across the rocks. I can't hear the man, but I run as if he's right behind me.

It feels like forever until I reach the path. I scramble up the snow bank and into the black woods. When I reach the cabin clearing, it is just a ghostly outline in the moonlight. I run to the steps and wrench open the door.

The candle burning on the hearth flickers. One of the candles that Mama and I made together. And he just left it burning. I run to blow it out then stop in my tracks.

Everything is different.

The three deerskins sewn together that we used as a covering are in a pile on the floor. Bed skins covered in a huge white square of fabric. Sacks are piled in the corner. I look closer. I recognize the reddish gold symbol on the top one. Flour. I lift it off. The bag underneath is lumpy and rough. As I shift it to get a better look, something rolls out of the top. A potato? He brought potatoes in a sack? How could he have this many left this late in the season? And they're perfect and round, not wrinkled at all like our spring potatoes.

I look at all the sacks. Some are sugar and rice. There is one filled with white powder that crumbles between my fingers which has a picture of a cow on it. I stand back and look at the pile again. All of the sacks would be enough to fill Uncle Samuel's boat to the rim. Why would the man bring so much? Why would he bring food into the cabin at all if he just wants to kill me?

I turn back to the hearth. The candle is still burning. A drop of wax runs from a melted pool at the top down the side, fast at first then slowly as it cools. How long have I been in here? The man could be back any time now.

Don't let them see you, Eve! Mama screams in my head.

I glance around. The cabin is full of the man's things. If he's coming back here, there's no place for me to go.

I can't stay in the cabin.

I'll have to go outside. Melted snow drips off my skirt, down my leg, and into my boot. My teeth are chattering. I snatch the skins from the floor and tuck them under my arm.

There is a pot on the stove. It must be the dinner that the man said he made. I lift the lid and peer into the pot. The handle is warm in my hand. A rich, salty, fatty smell engulfs my face. I could just take one spoonful. Just one mouthful of warm broth to slide down my throat.

He wants to kill me. Maybe that's what the food is for. I set the lid back down and step backwards. The last cranberry cake hangs above the stove. Its sourness wafts up my nose. I stuff it under my arm on top of the skins and run out of the cabin into the night.

The moon is the only light left. I hug the deerskins tighter against the cold. Where can I go?

"Where are you? Can you hear me?"

He's coming back. His voice sounds hoarse and tired. My legs want to run, but I don't know where. The light of the upside-down candle bobs through the trees. I've got to go somewhere.

"Can you see me? Where are you?"

I dart down the path to the meat cache and climb the ladder.

The man calls out again. I feel along the wall of the cache for the door. With the trees blocking the moonlight, I can't see anything. The light comes closer. My fingers run over the latch. I wrench it open, throw myself in and pull it shut behind me. The darkness swallows me, hides me, makes me invisible.

✺

Something cold digs into my body. I roll over. The deerskin slides off, leaving my skin exposed. I reach back to pull it back down. My fingers grope in the darkness for the other deerskin. My hand rams into a knot in one of the logs. Logs?

I sit up. My head whacks something cold and hard. I'm in the meat cache. Yesterday floods back.

The man is here. In our cabin.

I throw the deerskins off. My whole body screams as I move. The hard logs of the meat cache have grabbed onto my muscles, squeezing. I ease onto my knees. I peer through a space at the top of the door. Early morning light. The crack is angled so I can just see the corner of the porch.

I pull the deerskins around me. My hand squishes into the cranberry cake. I lick the pulp from my palm. It feels like I'm eating sour sawdust. But before I think about it, the whole cake is gone.

As soon as it's fully light, the man will be able to see the ladder of the meat cache. I have to go now. Before he gets up.

I roll the deerskin into a ball and shove it under my arm. I crawl to the opposite wall. My long underwear catches on a stob in the floor and rips. I run my fingers below the crack of light at the top of the door, looking for the latch. I find it with the side of my knuckles and push it open. It creeks so loudly I freeze halfway out the door.

I look over to the cabin in the grey light. There isn't any sign of the man, except for the boards that used to cover the windows in a pile on the porch.

The ladder clunks against the log as I go down. As soon as I reach the snow, I sprint off along the path. I don't know where I'm going. I'm just getting away from the man.

I break onto the beach. Light floods from across the water. I hug myself against it. There's nowhere to hide out here.

I need to be close enough to the cabin so I know where the man is. But I can't let him see me. My hiding spot! I'll be able to hear and watch everything he does. I'll know when he leaves. And there's no way he can see me through the dense trees. I slip back into the woods, deer skin wrapped tight against the cold.

I've only just barely ducked under the spruce branches when the fawn comes up behind me. Seeing him makes me want to laugh, cry and sing at the same time. But I can't make any sound at all. He nuzzles the back of my neck. I stroke his ears. I can feel his antler nubs poking up. He takes his head out from under my hand and sniffs at my pocket.

"I don't have anything for you, little guy."

He presses his nose against my pocket. I can feel the lichen that I harvested yesterday press into my thigh. He's just as hungry as I am.

I nudge the fawn's head away with my elbow and pull the lichen out of my pocket. It's dried out, all crinkly in my hand. I try to pull a single strand out of the ball but it crumbles in my fingers.

The fawn reaches his nose down and takes the lichen out of my hand. He eats it in three chews. Without me, he probably didn't get any food at all last night. I stroke his neck. The cabin door swings open.

From my hiding spot I can only see the man's back. Instead of the blue coat with the red things on the shoulders, he has on a brown wool coat, like Mama's and Uncle Samuel's and mine. His hair is rumpled, one tuft sticking straight up.

The fawn nudges at my pocket. I try not to move. The man cups his hands around his mouth and shouts towards the creek.

"Are you out there? Hey, are you all right?"

Am I all right? Am I out here? I clench my fist. I would be all right if he hadn't come. I would be warm. I would be able to feed the fawn. I could eat my own soup. I could sleep in my own bed. I could be alone.

And lonely.

The man turns around and looks towards my hiding place. I hold my breath. I know he can't see me through the spruce branches, but I squirm away from his eyes.

He lifts his hands up to his mouth again then lowers them. He talks so softly I can hardly hear him.

"I've made breakfast for you," he says. "You must be hungry after not eating dinner last night."

I can almost smell the warm fatty soup that was on the stove. My empty stomach grumbles. Could he have heard it? I think about the cranberry cake I chewed in the meat cache. The dry sourness still tight in my throat.

The man looks down at his feet. It doesn't seem like he's talking to me anymore. "I promised Sarah that I'd take care of you," he whispers. "I promised."

Sarah?

Does he mean Mama? He promised Mama he'd take care of me?

The man is standing still. He must have meant someone else. But I know he said Sarah. There can be more than one Mama or more than one brother, but there couldn't be more than one Sarah or Eve.

It doesn't matter what he says. I promised Mama not to let *him* even see me. She loved me. She took care of me.

The man goes inside the cabin, leaving the door open. I imagine all the heat rushing out. My legs want to run out of the trees, up the steps and catch some of that warmth. Just for a second. Just a tiny blast of warm on my numb fingers.

But I can't. I can't eat, I can't cut wood, I can't stay warm, I can't feed the fawn. If the man did promise to take care of me, he's broken it a thousand times already.

The fawn beds down in the snow three paces away.

"I'll always take care of you," I breathe. Curled in the snow, the fawn looks like he did when he was so afraid of me. When I fed him sugar on my mitten for the first time.

After I took away his Mama.

The man comes back out of the cabin carrying my bowl in one hand and Mama's in the other. I can see the steam rising in the cold. He stands on the steps and calls out towards the creek.

"I've got breakfast here for you." He stands on the porch, steam on either side of his face. I glare back at him through the wall of spruce branches. Finally he sets Mama's bowl on the porch.

"I'll just leave yours on the beach then." He walks down the path to the shore with mine.

"Dear god, she must be hungry," he says softly.

God? Who is he talking to?

As he walks past the meat cache, the soup's smell wafts over to me. It's just like last night, but somehow even better. I shouldn't eat it. But I didn't promise Mama anything about eating food. And now all I have is a dried ball of lichen.

I'm so hungry.

I can at least go and see where the man is putting it. I stand as quietly as I can and follow him.

I stand at the fringe of the trees by the beach. The man sets the bowl down on a rock then turns back down the trail. His boots squeak softly in the snow. I listen until I can't hear them anymore.

The thump of the cabin door is so soft, I'm not even sure it's there. The soup steams from its rock. I only promised Mama not to let him see me. I step out onto the beach.

My fingers cup the warm bowl. I take a sip. The broth is so thick it's almost like drinking deer fat. It's better than anything Mama ever made. Even on the nights when Samuel came with special meat that he said was just for a growing bear cub. I don't use the spoon the man left on the rock. Just drink it down until there isn't a drop left.

TWELVE

I can't go back to the meat cache.

He's waiting for me to go back there, waiting for me to eat his food. Which I should never have eaten in the first place. I look up through the spruce branches of my hiding place. I can barely see the plate, sitting outside the door of the cache. The smell carries all the way over to me. The fattiness. The warmth. If only he had left the plate on the beach like he has for the last five days.

I close my eyes and bite my lip. No. I won't let him lure me closer. That's what he wants. He's not feeding me to take care of me, he is doing it to make me come closer to the cabin. So he can catch me.

But why did he choose the meat cache? Was it just a spot closer to the cabin or does he know I'm sleeping there?

Rain drips from my hair under my collar and down my back. The melting snow plops out of the trees around me, leaving craters in the needle-laden snow. I pull my arms into my tunic. Even with the deerskin blanket wrapped around my shoulders, I'm shivering.

The man comes out on the porch and sits on the steps. Fear and cold anger mix and bubble up. He took Mama, the cabin, the meat cache. What can he take next? When will I have nothing left?

The rain makes the woods even darker than usual. The man eats his dinner hunched over Mama's bowl, his spoon barely moving a hand span between the food and his mouth. He doesn't talk to me. Not even to ask if I'm warm enough. Or talk about shoveling all the snow. He barely even looks up from his food.

My stomach grumbles. I turn away from the man and curl up under the deerskin at the base of the alders. My teeth chatter so hard my head shakes. No matter how hard I try to push it out of my mind, I picture the man's dinner. Steaming hot. Meat and salt and fat.

I hear the door close as the man returns to the cabin. I'm alone.

After dark, the fawn beds down next to me. He starts out three paces away but soon his back is pressed against my side. His warmth is more than all my layers put together. I wiggle my fingers out of the skin and put them on the back of his neck.

"I'll never let the man take *you* away," I whisper in his ear. "You're safe with me."

❦

Smoke from the man's morning fire curls down from the chimney, through the spruce branches onto the ground, drifting past me. My feet have fallen asleep from squatting so long. I hang on to the trunk of a young spruce to keep my balance. I close my eyes and imagine how warm it is in the cabin—the radiating wood stove, the dry bed skins. I dream of Mama. I hear her laugh and call me bear cub and wild child.

But now the man is there, drinking from our cups, burning the wood I cut on my own. He might be sitting on the bed right now, chewing on the last bit of our salmon He's taken everything. Even the meat cache.

I squeeze my hand tighter around the branch. Being angry only makes me colder. And I haven't been warm since he came. Nine nights, now.

The fawn walks up behind me. I relax. He sniffs my hands and then checks my pockets.

"I'm sorry little guy, I can't get sugar for you."

He headbutts my chest. I have to grab the branch again to keep from falling over. "Hey," I whisper, smiling. "We've got to be quiet." He rubs his head on my knee. We can make it a little longer.

The cabin door slams.

The man steps onto the porch and stares our way. He must have heard me laugh! I'm hidden by the spruce branches now but if he comes closer...if he turns off the porch and walks the ten paces towards me...The fawn turns around and trots into the woods. Every part of me wants to follow him, but it will make too much noise. The man stares straight at me. I hold as still as I can. "Look the other way," I beg in my head. "Please, look the other way."

Finally the man turns his head toward the creek. I slide my eyes to see where he is looking but I can't without moving my head. The man stares in that direction then slowly turns and goes inside the cabin. I breathe out a sigh of relief, and turn my head to see what he was looking at. The fawn has looped through the woods and come out of the trees by the creek. He walks across the yard towards the trees I'm hidden in. I smile. It seems like he just went over there to make the man look the other way.

The man closes the door so quietly that I don't realize that he's back outside until the bottom step creaks. I freeze again. He has a strange thing in his hand. It has a chunk of wood on one end and a long pole sticking out of the other. I can see a hole in the end of the pole. The man kneels, then lowers the stick and points it at the fawn.

The fawn is three paces from the trees where I'm hidden when he stops and turns towards the man. He flicks his tail, letting the white underneath show. Everything is still.

The air shatters. There is enough sound to make the cliffs collapse, to make every single tree in the valley crash to the ground. The fawn jumps straight up. Before his feet are back on the ground, he is running. He careens through the spruce branches. His legs fly in wild directions. His feet fold. He collapses five feet behind me. A trickle of blood runs down his chest into the moss.

I crawl toward him. A rim of white shows where his eyes are rolled back into his head. I slide my hands under his chest and lift the front of his body onto my lap. His muscles quiver.

Warm blood soaks into my thigh. He kicks his back legs. Sharp hoofs dig into my calves. I press my hand onto his back trying to hold him still. "It's okay," I whisper. But I know it's not. The fawn, my fawn, isn't there anymore. Only a kicking, dying, animal. I can feel his heart beating. When I lift my hand, deep crimson blood runs down my wrist.

He's looking up at me. I touch my fingers to his forehead leaving a drop of blood. He kicks again. I put my hand on his chest. "You're going to be all right," I whisper. His heart beats once. I hold my breath. Twice.

Then nothing.

I press my hands deeper into the fur, searching for his pulse. His eyes are lifeless. His chest still. My breath rushes out. Something tears in my chest. My fawn is dead. I suck in air, choking on an explosion of tears. He's dead. He's dead. He's dead. The words cut into me. Rip me apart. I bury my face into his neck.

His head slides down my thighs and off into the moss. His jaw is slack. I try to lift him back up but his head slumps to one side. The dead weight of his muscles are twice as heavy as they were two minutes ago. I let the body drop back into my lap. His neck is bent at an odd angle. His tongue hangs to one side.

"No!" I scream. "No, no, no!" Without trying to make the words come out I'm screaming and sobbing. Gasping and choking.

"No!"

I lift him up again, try to make his neck go straight. A mix of the cud he was chewing and red-black blood drips out his nose onto my sleeve. The blood on his chest has matted his fur. His eyes are glazed. He's not my fawn anymore. Just a dead deer.

"I'm so sorry," the man says.

My heart stops. I turn my head. His boots are inches from me.

"I didn't realize he..." he pauses. "I didn't know that you knew him."

He kneels down next to me. His eyes are shiny and wet. A tear rolls down his cheek. His face is right where Mama's was when they searched the cabin. The scraggly hair on the man's jaw shifts. Mama's there, Mama's beside me, crying.

Promise you won't let them see you, Eve. She leans in closer. I reach out to hug her, to tell her I promise, but the man is there again.

"I broke my promise, Mama," I whisper.

"I won't hurt you," the man says. "It's all right."

"You'll kill me!" I shout. I push the fawn's body off my legs. I might have let him see me, but I won't let him catch me.

I stand and push through the brush. The spruce branches grab me, trying to hold me back. I break through and start to run, tripping and stumbling. My legs are wobbly from sitting so long. I scamper under the meat cache and turn down the path to the beach. The man's boots clomp behind me. I can't let him catch me.

I break out of the trees and stumble over the rocks. *He'll kill you*, says Mama. *You didn't pay attention. You never should have fed the fawn. I told you it would kill him.* I sprint down the shore to where the waves crash on the low tide.

I'm sorry, Mama! I yell back in my head. Wind roars in my ears.

You broke your promise, Eve, you broke your promise.

I run even faster. My heart pounds in my head. The beach bends under me. The mud! I swerve up the beach to firmer ground.

I dash over the rocks. Gulp in air. My throat is too small to fit enough in. I teeter and slip. I won't let him catch me. I won't let him catch me. I won't let him.

"Wait!" he calls. I glance over my shoulder, trip, and fall flat.

The little air I have left is knocked out. He'll catch me now. I'm going to die. He's going to kill me. *I'm sorry, Mama, I'm so sorry. I cut my hair. I stole the sugar. I broke my promise. I killed the fawn.* Waves crash against the shore. This is what Mama said would happen.

I don't mind anymore, now that the fawn is dead.

A rock is jabbing into my stomach. The man will be here any second. With his stick. I squeeze my eyes shut tight. And wait.

I can't hear the man. I push myself up. Waves break against the rocks. Something thrashes at the water's edge. I stand.

The man is buried up to his knees in the mud flat. Gulls circle over the cove calling to each other through the rain. He flails and squirms, sinking deeper. A wave crashes two paces behind him on the incoming tide.

The man arches his back, trying to break free. The mud only pulls harder.

THIRTEEN

Mud sprays up around the man as he struggles. It swallows him slowly, past his knees, sliding up his thighs. He flings his arms around in circles, then falls forward. One arm is stuck up to his elbow.

My legs walk towards him without my telling them to. Somehow my feet find a way through the rocks. My knees wobble. I don't take my eyes off the man's back, not even when I slip on the seaweed.

The rocks start to bend under me. I back up. The man tries to turn his head towards me but he's stuck facing the other way.

Don't let them see you, Eve! My legs freeze. Ready to turn around and run. A wave crashes, spray hitting my skirt. I jump back. The man recoils and turns his face away from the water. The wave soaks his legs and chest.

I circle the man, moving back up around the mud. Where he can see me.

The man's arm is buried up to his shoulder now. His face is sideways, the top of his head almost touching the mud. His eyes lock on mine. They're bright blue. Even brighter than Uncle Samuel's. They are wild like the doe's, panicked like the fawn's, in the moments before they died.

I should say something. Do something. I stand and stare.

The man struggles, straining every muscle in his body to get free. His eyes leave mine.

"Don't move," I call into the wind. "You'll only sink deeper."

The man stops thrashing and looks up at me again. "I'm sorry," he says. "About everything. I didn't take care of you. I broke my promise to Sarah. I made a mess of everything."

His promise. I pull at the straggled wet ends of my hair. He really did promise Mama.

"I broke my promise, too," I whisper.

Only when the man's eyes widen do I realize that I said it out loud.

The wind blows a gust of rain sideways, slapping my side. I stumble.

"You should go back to the cabin," the man says. "You shouldn't be out here."

I look back at him one more time. Then turn and run up the beach.

I let the doe die, I killed the fawn, I made Mama leave.

My foot catches on something hard. Peeking out from the kelpline is the pile of boards Mama and I used to dig out the dead doe. I kneel down.

The man is all that's left on the Island. Without him, I'll be completely alone. I look back. He's a dot on the edge of the incoming tide.

The tide doesn't wait.

I grab the board on top of the pile and yank it out from under the snow. The wood is splintery. I see my hands start to bleed. I'm too cold to feel anything. I grip the rough, waterlogged wood as tightly as I can and haul it out of the grass.

I turn and drag the board down the beach. It bounces over the rocks, jerking in my hands. The man is still struggling, sinking deeper.

"Don't move!" I call through the wind. I'm too far for him to hear me.

The plank lodges itself between two rocks. I go back to wrestle it out.

The man turns, trying to look at me. I move faster. The easiest way to get to him is on the side towards the water, but it's covered up by the tide.

I'll have to go through the mud the long way to save him.

The seaweed is thick and slippery. I reach the edge of the mud. He looks at me and starts to say something but stops. I shove the board towards him. The end plows into clay.

"Can you reach it?" I ask.

He stares at me. There are streaks of wet on his face—tears or rain, I can't tell. The blue of his eyes seems even brighter. He's not like Samuel or like Mama, but now his face is familiar.

He reaches as far as he can and shakes his head. The board is still an arm's length away.

"I'll have to go get another one," I call. The man nods. I think that I hear him shout something as I run up the beach, but I don't even turn.

The boards are coated in muddy ice. I kneel and wrap my fingers around them and try to pull up. They're stuck. Another splinter lodges itself in my palm.

The wind slashes me with rain. I'm pushed sideways. I wriggle the toe of my boot underneath the corner of the board, shove my fingers beneath the front edge and pry up. The board lifts six inches and then falls back onto my foot. I yelp and fall backwards, my foot still pinned.

I could go back to the cabin. That's what Mama would want. That's what the man wants, too. And I tried to save him.

I look down at my hands, white with cold, blood mixing with the rain. I tried. I just can't lift this last board. I'm cold and weak. The man took too much from me. I can't save him.

I rip my foot from under the board and push myself up. He's the reason all of this happened. I'm sick of doing what he tells me. I jam my hands back under the board and pry up. The grass rips and pops. I push harder than I need to, sending the board shooting up. I snap my arms back and let it fall onto the beach.

I could go back. Just turn up the path, walk up through the snow, into the warm cabin. I could be safe. From the man. From the tide. From everything. I look down the beach. The man is just a spot on the water's edge. His red hair framed by the grey black water and rocks.

The tide doesn't wait.

I pick up the last board and start down the rocks.

The man's eyes are on me as I lug the board towards him. He's finally stopped thrashing. I'm not afraid of him anymore. The only thing to fear is the water, the mud, the cold.

I ease my foot onto the rough board. It sinks with my weight. I step forward again, the mud rising around my ankles. Rain pushes me sideways. The rocks wobble. One step off and we'll both be stuck here. We'll both drown with the tide. I inch my feet closer to the man, closer to the sea.

I pull the second plank from behind me and keep moving.

Step by step, I get to the end of the first board. I'm so close to the man. So close we could almost touch. But he's still so far away.

I pull the second plank from behind me until it's almost straight up in the air. My arms shake as I try to hold it up. Waves slap the man's body, surging around him, hissing back out, surging again. He gasps and coughs between swells. Purple creeps around his lips.

"I promised Sarah that I'd take care of you," he says. "Not that you'd risk your life for me."

I shuffle further out on the board. All that matters is saving the man. It doesn't matter what he thinks. It doesn't matter what Mama thinks. All that matters is him. All that matters.

A bigger set of waves rolls in, breaking over the man's head. His hair is soaked. His face streaked with dirt.

I let go of the board and push it forward. It smacks down in front of the man, spraying water and muck. It reaches. The man just looks at me. The rain and waves tear between us.

"Push!" I yell.

He doesn't move.

"Put your weight on the board. You have to get out." My voice is high and shrill. My teeth are chattering so hard that the man is blurry. I see him lean forward and push himself up. See his muscles strain, see him rise slowly out of the clay. See the swell pounding around him in an angry white mass.

My end of the board jerks as the man puts his full weight on it. My body tips off. The angry water shifts to angry sky, full of circling gulls and rain. I feel the mud

sucking my legs and arms down. Feel my eyes close without me telling them to.

And then I feel nothing.

FOURTEEN

The wood stove door squeaks open. Mama moves softly around the cabin. From the stove to the wood box. To the door. To kneeling by the bed. The bed is soft underneath me. I breathe in its sweet scent. Mama reaches out and lays her hand on my forehead.

Rain pounds on the roof. The trees moan in the wind.

Samuel bounces his bow over all of the fiddle strings, then plays a long A. I listen to him tune, the pitch moving up and down until it finds the perfect smooth note in the middle. I roll over and snuggle into the warm, dry deerskins.

Samuel stops playing.

"Are you awake?" he asks.

The voice is too high.

I open my eyes. The man.

He kneels on the floor. One hand on the bed, one holding Samuel's fiddle. His red hair is ruffled, backlit by the sun. Dried mud clings to his scraggly beard. "Are you all right?" he asks. "Are you still cold?"

I look at his blue eyes. The wrinkles on his forehead look like Mama's when she was worried. In his hands, the fiddle looks as good as new, the bridge back in place, the crack just a faint scar. The wood is polished, even down to the stain from the rosin beneath the neck.

It's perfect.

The man turns to the stove and then back to me.

"I've got water for tea. Do you want some?"

I push myself up so I'm leaning on my elbow. I'm wearing Mama's shirt, not the muddy one I had before.

Why is he taking care of me?

I remember the storm. The rain. The gulls. The tide. The mud.

I saved him. I saved the man.

He hands me a steaming cup of tea. I sit up and take it from him. I have so many questions. Why did he feed me? Why did he chase me? Why did he take Mama? But I don't know how to ask.

"Thank you," he says. "You saved my life."

Steam from the tea wafts up and condenses on my face. I saved him. The last board worked. It was enough for him to push himself out.

But he brought me here. He must have pulled me out of the mud, carried me up the beach. I saved his life, but he saved mine, too.

He's looking at me. I don't know what to do. Don't know what to say. Finally, I look from my tea to his face.

"How did you fix the fiddle?" I ask.

The man looks startled, then glances down at the fiddle as if to be sure he actually did fix it. Then he launches into a torrent of words.

"I learned how to do repairs when I first met Samuel. He had a late night gig at a bar, and he played so well it made me want to learn, but I couldn't play to save my life. So I started out learning on how to fix the instruments themselves. And then I became friends with Samuel, who tried for years to teach me how to play."

The man keeps his eyes on the fiddle. I don't know what a gig is. Or a bar. But he knew Samuel. They were friends.

"Why did you come here?" I ask. "Why did you take Mama?"

He turns away from me. The fire crackles, orange flame sending light out from a thin place in the stack. I curl my fingers around my tea cup, warmth tingling up my arms.

"I came here to find Sarah because I missed her," he finally says. "But after I took her back home, I knew that I had made a mistake about the whole society."

He pauses. Light streams through the uncovered windows. I knew he took Mama, but somehow having him say it makes it worse. He took Mama back home. He thought Mama had another home. Suddenly, I don't want to hear any more. I don't want to know. I want to shield my eyes. Go back to sleep.

"But it was too late," he keeps going. " I couldn't bring Sarah back, I couldn't free Samuel. You were all I had left." He picks up Samuel's fiddle again and polishes it, moving the cloth in tiny, gentle circles just above the chin rest.

"I knew Sarah was still alive after she escaped. I just had this feeling. Even after the search party had given up. So when Samuel got back three days late from a 'fishing trip' last spring, I knew he was up to something. When he left again in the fall, I followed him. Not closely, just enough to know he stopped on St. James Island." He turns the fiddle over and starts polishing the back. "After I told the authorities, things spun out of control. They threw Samuel in jail. They sent twelve armed men out in the search boat to get Sarah. There was nothing I could do."

The heat radiating off the stove warms my cheeks. He followed Samuel. Last spring when he stayed for three days. That's what Mama and Samuel were afraid of in the fall. That's why Samuel left in the storm.

But it was already too late.

He stops polishing the fiddle. "I'm so sorry."

I don't know what to say back. "Is *this* St. James Island?" I ask.

The man turns back to me with the stove door half-way open. "Yes." He looks confused. "Or at least that's what I've always called it."

I nod. The stove crackles.

The man turns the damper down with his toe. "But when I took Sarah back to the society, it was all wrong. I'd always thought the society was a good thing. I thought it eliminated suffering, just like I'd been trained to think. Samuel and Sarah were the only ones who ever told me anything different, and I didn't believe them until it was too late."

Dust swirls in the sunlight. The man pauses, watching everything but me. His hands are still holding the fiddle in his lap. Red scratches from the boards cover his palms. He runs one hand over his cheek, knocking chunks of dried mud from his beard stubble onto his coat.

"Sarah and Samuel wouldn't even talk to me. I begged for hours at the jail and the enclosure, just for them to tell me something about you. I told them that I'd been wrong. But they wouldn't even tell me your name." He stops. The only noise is the gentle rush of the creek. Even the fire is perfectly quiet. Everything seems to be waiting.

I twist my fingers around a strand of hair hanging in front of my face.

"I'm Eve," I say.

The man lays Samuel's fiddle across his lap. "Of course that's what she would have named you," he whispers.

"Why?"

He puts his hand on the fiddle and traces the curve of the scroll with his first finger; in and out, in and out.

"Eve was the woman who helped Sarah when she first came to the enclosure. She was like her second mother. They loved each other so much. And she always told Sarah that one day they would all be free. But she died a year before Sarah escaped. Before we…before she got pregnant."

The man stops tracing the scroll. There was another person who took care of Mama. Who loved her. Who I never knew about.

I twist my fingers in the fur of the bed skins. There are probably more things that Mama never told me. I chew on my lip. There was a whole world that she left behind. And the man left it, too.

"Why did you come back here again?" I ask.

The man moves his jaw back and forth. More mud falls into his lap. "You're the only person I have left. The only good piece of the mess of the society. But I was afraid all I would find was your body."

The man stops again and clears his throat. His voice gets higher. "And when I saw your red hair go running down the beach the first night, it was the happiest, saddest, and most terrifying moment of my life." He stops and brushes something off his cheek. A raven croaks.

"I'm your father, your Papa, but I didn't know it until I came the first time. I didn't know I had a daughter all these years."

I bring my eyes up to his.

"I'm probably the worst Papa that ever lived," he whispers.

He is my Papa. The words feel funny just to think. Papa.

All the time I was alone, he was thinking about me. He was trying to come back. And I spent all this time hiding from him, all this time alone, when I could have had the fire, and food. I was by myself under the spruce trees when I could have been warm and dry. I could've had part of what things were like before they took Mama.

The man wraps his fingers around the neck of Samuel's fiddle and rests the bottom on his leg, then turns it slowly. The polished wood gleams in the sun. Each time he turns the instrument, light glints off the strings. I watch him, then set my empty tea cup on the hearth.

"Do you want more tea?" he asks.

I nod. He hands me the fiddle then reaches down to scoop more water into the pot. The cup clunks into the empty bottom.

"I'll go out to the creek to get some more water," he says.

"I can help." I put Samuel's fiddle down and push myself up.

"No, it's all right." He stands quickly. "You should rest. You've been outside for days."

I open my mouth to say something, but then close it again and slide on my boots. They are still caked in clay, but the man had turned them so they dried by the fire. The warm felt on the inside hugs my feet.

He waits for me and I walk out the door with him. The snow has melted even more in the night, showing brown green earth on the logs. The clouds are higher than I've seen them for weeks.

We reach the creek. The man pushes the bucket down to the creek bottom, scrunching against the gravel. Current ripples out in a V on either side. Water only covers the opening halfway.

"Here." I take the bucket from him. "It's deeper down here."

I dip it into the water hole. When it's as full as it can get without it spilling, I hoist it out. The man grabs the handle and lifts, too. As we step out of the water, his boots splash water at my knees. I splash water at him from the bucket.

He turns, startled. Then he flicks water back at me. I grin and I splash back. He sets down the bucket, and slaps the top, sending a wall of water at me. It soaks my coat and drips down into my warm dry boots.

"Oh...I..." He looks shocked, as I stand there dripping. "Sorry, that was more water than I meant."

I jump into the creek, ignoring the cold as the water floods into my boots. I splash as much as I can up the bank, dousing his whole back.

"Hey!" He shouts, grinning. He picks up the whole bucket and tries to pour it at me, but most of it runs onto his feet. I dash out of the creek and towards the cabin, with him chasing behind me, water sloshing everywhere. He gets the last cup down my neck, just before I reach the door of the cabin.

We stand there looking at each other, the empty water bucket between us. I giggle. He laughs back. I take off my coat and ring it out. The puddle drains out between the cracks in the boards.

The man chuckles. "That's a lot of water."

I nod. "I know, we might as well have gone swimming."

He laughs. Then pulls off his boots, water oozing from his socks.

"Sarah would have thought we were crazy," he says, ringing out his boot liners. "Trying to do something useful, and we'd come back soaking wet with an empty water bucket."

I can just imagine Mama's face, annoyed and laughing at the same time.

"What about Samuel and Mama?" I ask. "When are they coming back?"

The man slowly sets his wet boots down. The smile drains from his face.

"They can't come back. Eve, I...I don't know how they could. Samuel is in jail. Sarah's back in the enclosure. And even if she did escape, this is the first place they would look for her."

They can't come back.

The words pound over and over in my head. *They can't come back.* I run my fingers over the patch in my shirt that Mama sewed. I stare at the neglected, dried and cracking pile of roots on the porch that Mama was starting to weave into a basket. The cabin is full of memories of Mama. All stopped. *They can't come back.* Frozen. And now they never will be finished.

I hate the man again. I dig my fingers into the soggy wool of my coat and shake with anger. I don't care if he's my father. I don't care how sorry he is. I hate him. He took Mama and she can never come back. I hate him.

"I'm so sorry," the man says.

I look up. He's crying.

"I'm so sorry, Eve."

I unknot my fingers from my coat, letting it fall to the porch. A tear drips off the man's cheek into his beard. My throat tightens as I start to cry, too. Mama and Samuel are gone.

Forever.

Just like the fawn.

I run to him and bury my face in his coat. He wraps his arms around my shoulders. We're both crying. For Mama. For Samuel. For everything we lost. For each other.

"I'm so sorry," he keeps saying.

Finally, I let go of Papa's shoulders. I wipe my eyes.

"I'm going to go see the fawn," I say.

He almost jumps. "Eve, the fawn's..."

"I know. He's dead. I'm just going to go see him."

"All right," he says. "If you're sure that's what you want to do."

I pull on my coat and boots again, still soaked, then go down the steps.

I turn behind the cabin pushing the spruce branches back from the wall. Papa stays a few steps behind me, still in his wet socks. The fawn's body is stiff on the moss, his neck bent backward, hoofs curled in. Black blood is congealed on his chest and face.

I sink onto my knees. His eyes are glossy and cold. The man rests his hand on my shoulder.

I want to bury my face in the fawn's fur. Want to stroke his forehead, want to feel his soft, wet nose. But he's just a cold body. Just like any other deer. I knot my hands in my coat pockets.

Slowly, the man kneels next to me.

"Do you want to bury him?" he asks quietly.

I take my hand out of my pocket and lay it gently on the cold fur. "Tomorrow morning. At low tide."

❦

The tide is out just far enough that we can walk onto the reef. The swell is still big, but the waves roll by without whitecaps, tired out from last night's storm. The clouds are so high I can pretend they're not there. It's almost spring.

The man carries the fawn in his arms, walking a few paces behind me. The fawn is rigid, his legs sticking out at an awkward angle. The man follows me through the tide pools on the narrow bar connecting the reef to shore. Waves slap against the rocks, and then rush out again. We walk to the point farthest out in the channel, sending a hauled-out sea otter crashing back into the water.

"Right here?" the man asks.

I shake my head. "Down here by the water."

He lays the body gently on the rocks. I reach into my pocket and pull out the last handful of sugar from the sack Samuel brought. My coat pocket is sticky from all the times I've carried sugar in it. I kneel next to the fawn and put the sugar in his mouth. His lips and tongue are cold and stiff. The man just watches.

I brush my hands off and stand. "Let's go back."

The man nods. I look at the fawn one last time then turn back towards shore. He walks with me. Wind has made his ears pink. He's wearing his brown wool coat just like the one Samuel wore.

When we reach the narrow bar that connects the reef to the island, we move into single file, the man in front. Just as we reach the shore I hear them. The soft chortling call, faint over the swell's rush. I look out over the water until I find the V of birds flying right over the channel, straight towards us.

"Cranes!" I shout, running to the water's edge. The man follows. We stand side by side as they fly towards us, morphing in and out of formation, calling back and forth. They fly over the ridge and back out over the water. We turn and watch until the flock is nothing but a speck in the grey clouds.

"I'd never really looked at the cranes when they flew through before," the man says.

"They flew over...the society?"

He nods. "Every spring and every fall. I just never paid that much attention. Sarah would notice, though. When the cranes were flying, those were the only times she would look truly happy. When she seemed to forget she was locked in the enclosure."

"Are these the same? The same birds will fly over Samuel and Mama?"

"I guess so. Yes, they'd have to be."

"Where else do they go?"

The man stops and runs his hands over his red beard. He keeps his eyes on the shifting V of birds.

"I'm not sure. But they stop to nest in the north, and then in the fall, they go back down south, to winter in the wheat fields. I guess Samuel would know more."

"Can you tell me about it sometime, Papa?" The word rolls out of my mouth without me thinking about it. The same way Mama talked about her papa.

He looks down at me, startled. Then his eyes glisten with tears. "Of course," he says. "Sometime, Eve, we'll go there. We'll find the other cabins on the north side of the island. Maybe someday, the society will change and we can go all the way back."

Papa looks back down at me. "But for now, we're going to make this work."

Behind us, the swell washes in and out, in and out. Somewhere on the cliffs, a raven calls. I stare at the patch of sky where the cranes disappeared. The world on the other side of the ridge is opening up underneath them. The island is the same as it always has been. And somewhere over the ridge, the cranes are still flying.

Photo by Iris White

LINNEA LENTFER was six weeks old when she first boated to Tàaś Daa, an island in Southeast Alaska. She returned each fall to hunt and explore with family and friends. Between annual Island visits, Linnea lived in Gustavus playing music, gardening, and reading. She moved to Juneau for high school where she ran cross country, skied and deepened her commitment to climate activism. Linnea's sense of place and community inspired her to write *Hold the Tide*, finishing her first draft at thirteen and final draft at sixteen. She completed high school in the spring of 2021 and is excited to attend Carleton College in the fall.